INTERVIEW PREPERATION TO DATA SCIENTIST ROLE

AN EMERGING PROFILE

PRASHANT RAWAT

ISBN 979-888546463-5

To the God....

Contents

Foreword *vii*

Preface *ix*

Acknowledgements *xi*

Prologue *xiii*

1. Chapter 1 1
2. Chapter 2 6
3. Chapter 3 18
4. Chapter 4 23
5. Chapter 5 31
6. Chapter 6 74

Foreword

"Great work, it will help data scientist enthusiast during their interview for data science roles"

"Data science students always keen about interview question patterns and well-structured answers. The textbook will provide them a great platform to make them interview ready. This is one of the exhaustive work done by Prof. Prashant Rawat and Dr. Prasenjit Model"

Preface

Hi reader, I am Prof. Prashant Rawat, wrote this book with extra zeal to simplify unnecessary mental complexity in data science related interview, generally faced by interviewees.

Data scientists and related personalities always curious about question answers trends in interviews. The ways to give diplomatic answers about job location, packages, office timings, languages are always a great concerns by all data scientists. The book provides state of the art answers and tricks, which ultimately resolve the issues. A wide range of actual interview stories also discussed for better understanding of tackling interviews.

Acknowledgements

I express my sincere acknowledgement to my parents for their constant love and support at every stages of my life. I especially thankful to my wife *(Priya Rawat)* and my son *(Adhvik Rawat)* for their love, understanding, support and cooperation. I am grateful to my co-author *(Dr Prasenjit Model)* and my organization *(University of Petroleum and Energy Studies)* for helping me during writing the book.

Prologue

Machine Learning's growth has confirmed our conviction that there isn't enough easily accessible education about this intriguing and rapidly growing topic.

When working with machine learning professionals to design the course and interacting with eager learners, we noticed a variety of sites that discuss ML job interviews, but no complete advice. There were individual profiles and collections of interview questions, but no comprehensive resource with solutions, no profiles that addressed the question of "how do I get this job?"

The purpose of this guide is to walk you through the full process of finding and securing a machine learning job, whether as an engineer, analyst, product manager, data scientist, researcher, or whatever role you decide is best for you.

We spoke with hiring managers and job seekers, on both sides of the table, to get a feel of what this experience and the job market, in general, are like right now. We wanted to talk to recruiters who locate candidates, hiring managers who conduct interviews and make offers and successful candidates who had gotten through rigorous machine learning interviews.

Thousands of people have learned the data science and machine learning skills they need to change careers and secure meaningful jobs in multiple MNCs. We have a broad network of students, alumni, and mentors, giving us a unique insight into the machine learning interview process.

A career in machine learning requires a considerable financial investment and is not without its hurdles. However, the payoff is enormous. AI and machine learning have been touted as the century's biggest breakthroughs. AI has the potential to revolutionize banking, health care, education, and a slew of other areas.

Making the decision to pursue a career as a machine learning engineer is a significant step in future-proofing your career.

So you're interested in artificial intelligence and machine learning. But how can you transform your passion into a profession? Let's get started.

CHAPTER ONE

What are AI, Machine Learning, and Deep Learning?

This part is for you if you're new to the subject, say as a programmer or analyst, and want to brush up on important terms and definitions of AI, machine learning, and deep learning.

Artificial Intelligence

Artificial intelligence has been present since the 1950s, but it has only recently become commonplace. Amazon, Facebook, and Google, companies with whom we engage on a daily basis, have all completely adopted AI. It's what keeps our product recommendations, maps, and social media feeds running. However, AI is used in goods by companies other than IT giants. AI solutions are being integrated by startups, banks, consulting firms, and even governments.

Artificial intelligence, to put it simply, is a machine that replicates human behavior in some way. AI can make engaging with a computer feel like interacting with a human. The output is the human part. Huge volumes of data are used as input. It's because of this that AI can learn and adapt. It processes massive amounts of data and information. When it comes across an issue, it learns from it and recognizes a pattern.

Artificial intelligence is described using a variety of concepts, some of which are interchangeable and others of which are erroneous. AI is a broad word that encompasses a variety of learning techniques. Machine learning, deep learning, and neural networks are the three main categories.

Here's a simple illustration to remember:

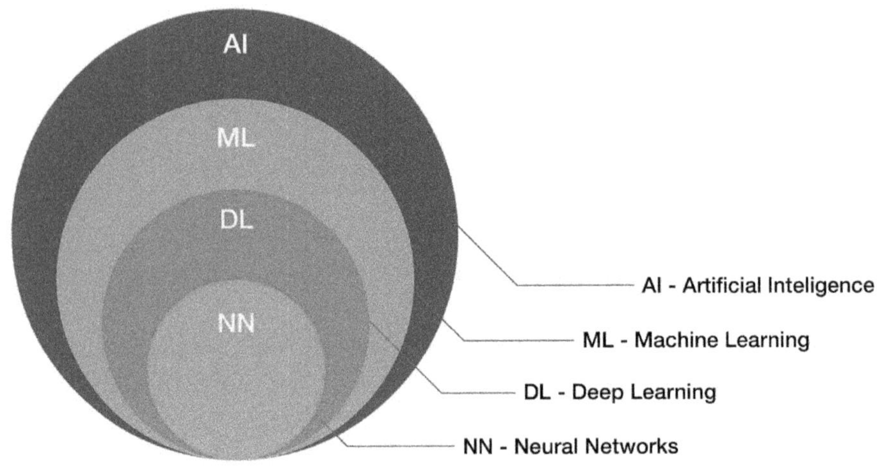

Generalized overview of data science domain

Machine Learning

Machine learning is a subset of artificial intelligence. It's a collection of approaches that allow computers to learn without having to be explicitly programmed to do so. One example is image classification: in a very naive interpretation, a computer could automatically identify pictures of apples and oranges and place them in different folders. And as more data is collected, the system will improve its performance.

Andrew Ng, a pioneer of current AI, has put together a handy table showing what machine learning can do:

What Machine Learning Can Do
A simple way to think about supervised learning.

INPUT A	RESPONSE B	APPLICATION
Picture	Are there human faces? (0 or 1)	Photo tagging
Loan application	Will they repay the loan? (0 or 1)	Loan approvals
Ad plus user information	Will user click on ad? (0 or 1)	Targeted online ads
Audio clip	Transcript of audio clip	Speech recognition
English sentence	French sentence	Language translation
Sensors from hard disk, plane engine, etc.	Is it about to fail?	Preventive maintenance
Car camera and other sensors	Position of other cars	Self-driving cars

SOURCE ANDREW NG

The overall working of the machine learning domain

Deep Learning and Neural Networks

Deep learning is a kind of machine learning that allows computers to learn and solve increasingly complicated patterns and problems. Natural language processing, which enables Chabot's and voice assistants like Siri, is one of the clearest uses of deep learning. Deep learning, which was only recently introduced, has been the main force behind the AI explosion.

Deep learning is based on neural networks, which are a type of machine learning that uses multiple layers of artificial neurons to simulate the human brain. Multi-layered neural networks with more neurons and interconnectedness are more powerful. Although neural networks have been studied for many years, they have just lately been taken to the next level and commercialized.

In terms of concept, here's how a simple neural network compares to a multi-layered neural network in deep learning:

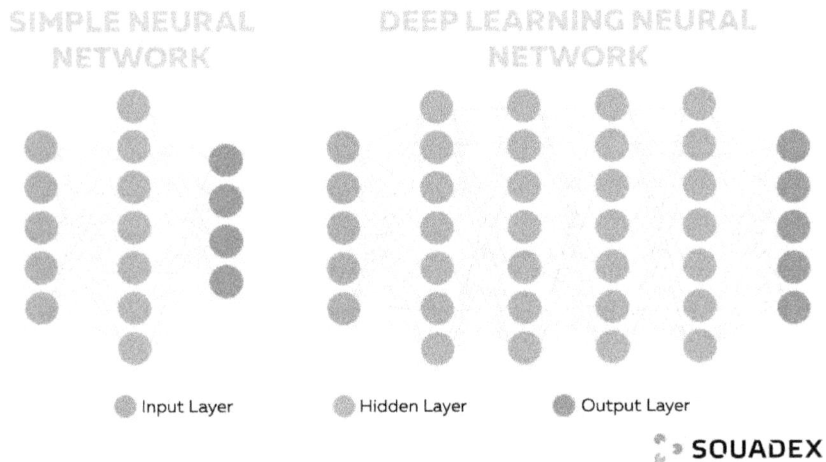

The general architecture of deep neural networks

It's critical to remember that these are broad, simplistic definitions. Each of these concepts could be defined differently by different organizations. They can also have different notions about how much depth they want from an application. This can be tough for candidates because job and interview requirements can be very different.

To identify what you'll need to know, I recommend supplementing the technical component of this book by searching for information about the company you're interested in. It is quite reasonable to carry out the following actions:

- Read as much as you can about the company to get a sense of what kind of AI it employs and how technical it is.
- Check Glassdoor to see if any employees have given information concerning job interviews and/or the company's general character.
- Look for ML-related employees on LinkedIn and examine their level of experience. If they all have a Ph.D. in computer science or statistics, for example, the organization may have a sophisticated, in-depth view of artificial intelligence.

- Contact the company directly, possibly through HR or a current member of the machine learning team. There's no harm in asking for further information.

Artificial Intelligence and Machine Learning Profile

Within the machine learning business, there are numerous roles to be filled. I'll outline the important areas you could work in and the most typically associated roles in this book:

- A machine learning engineer is the most prevalent type of engineer. You're in charge of the majority of coding apps. You build data-moving platforms and put data scientists' algorithms into action.
- You could work as a data analyst or a data scientist in the field of data science. Your task is to build data distinctions using machine learning models.
- Business Intelligence: You assist in the querying and presentation of business consequences, which are usually derived from data-driven insights.
- While the other roles are more applicable, a research scientist is more likely to push the boundaries of artificial intelligence by making new discoveries rather than using existing algorithms and models.
- Finally, there are positions such as product manager or lead for machine learning. In order to produce the product, this person brings together technology, business, and design. They're often in charge of assisting product creation and even controlling a product's profit and loss.

CHAPTER TWO

AI and ML Careers in Industries

Before we get into specific professions, let's take a look at the industries that use AI and machine learning professionals.

Various industries focus on different areas of knowledge and have unique requirements, languages, and data types. A software company, for example, will be more concerned with metrics than a bank. Code-switching, which is not a reference to computer programming but to the language and important terms that you express yourself in, is one of the key ways to keep in mind. Different businesses have their own lingo and knowing it might help you communicate effectively and land a job. It can specifically assist you in passing screening tests.

If you want to work in a specific field, you should use keywords that are more frequent in that industry in your resume and LinkedIn profile. It's crucial for the purposes of screening.

Software, higher education, and consulting/finance firms are the top hiring industries for machine learning, artificial intelligence, and data science skills, according to LinkedIn's Emerging Jobs Report. These industries, it turns out, also pay the most for machine learning talent. Different industries also place a greater emphasis on specific types of employment. Software, pharmaceutical, and telecommunications companies, for example, are often the main employers of data scientists. Aerospace and information technology industries, on the other hand, employ more engineers. Analysts are frequently engaged by healthcare, consultancy, and financial firms.

It's crucial to understand the industry in which your potential employers work so you can learn more about their demands and how they communicate.

Companies Opinion on AI and Machine Learning

Different companies may conduct interviews in a variety of ways. In general, we can divide businesses into three categories:

Machine Learning Product for Beginners

The dream: working with a tiny team in Silicon Valley, raising millions of dollars, and transforming the world. Working with an early-stage startup offers a lot more than just bragging rights. For one thing, you might be able to work the fastest within one and achieve a lot of accomplishment in a short length of time.

If you join an early-stage startup, one thing to keep in mind is that your job description will most likely change. You'll almost certainly be expected to undertake a variety of tasks in a variety of areas. You'll also need to be self-motivated, resourceful, and flexible because you'll most likely be short on resources.

Another thing to remember when starting a business is that the front-loaded nature of your efforts may be quite significant. You won't have a lot of existing data to work within most cases. Furthermore, if you want to leverage other people's data for your own machine learning products, you'll need to demonstrate a high level of reliability, security, and utility early on, all of which might be challenging for a small business (versus a larger company that has a lot of its own data or pre-existing relationships with customers). It's also worth thinking about whether the co-founders are distinctive and forward-thinking AI experts.

In a startup, you could have a once-in-a-lifetime opportunity, not only in terms of learning but also in terms of possible financial gain. However, like with most new enterprises, there's a good chance it'll fail.

Software Engineer, Machine Learning

APPLY FOR THIS JOB

SAN FRANCISCO ENGINEERING - MACHINE LEARNING FULL-TIME

Programmers spend too much time doing repetitive work – copying and pasting from StackOverflow, fixing simple errors, and writing boilerplate code. We're building an AI code engine that does this work for you. Programming using Kite is faster and more fun.

Kite is well-funded by top investors in Silicon Valley, including the founders of PayPal, Stripe, Palantir, and Dropbox to name a few. We are looking to expand our 15-person startup with talented individuals who are interested in joining an early stage startup. The ideal candidate is excited to help guide the direction of our product and company. They will have a significant amount of ownership of critical technical components. Our team is growing rapidly and we hope you'll grow with us too!

We are looking for a talented Software Engineer with experience writing production level code and has the infrastructure background to implement our cutting-edge models. If you have a strong background in software engineering and either have experience with machine learning or a willingness to learn, come join the team that's changing the way people code.

Machine Learning job profile opening

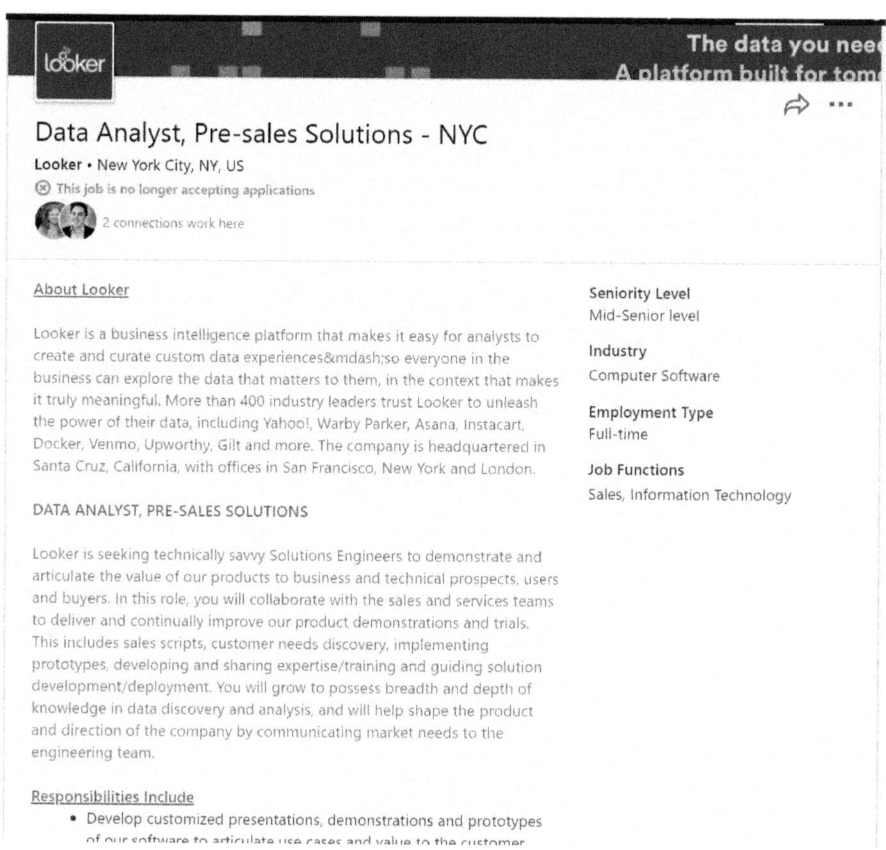

Data Analyst job profile opening

Mid-Cap Companies Data Leverages

On the hype cycle, AI and machine learning are still relatively new, but a number of firms have developed sizable data sets that can be used to incorporate ML into their operations. They can then use those data sets to improve their current goods as well as potentially generate new ones.

Every business with data is understanding that maximizing its value is a critical priority. However, many businesses are still working out how to do so. A frequent technique is to form an inside startup team capable of turning data into insights and, eventually, new products for the company. Most businesses recognize that using their data is critical to staying competitive.

As a result, if you're looking for a machine learning job with a midsize to large organization, you'll know you've got a good case to make.

Mid- to large-sized businesses will have more inflexible cultures and procedures in place, making it more difficult to innovate. However, you'll have data to work with, and you'll be able to create machine learning models based on millions of data points. You also know that, given the number of users and customers you're going to have, you have an opportunity to make an instant impact at scale.

While some of these organizations may not be at the forefront of machine learning or AI research, they still provide an excellent learning environment, as well as competitive salaries and benefits, as well as a solid basis on which to build.

Capital One, JP Morgan, Morgan Stanley, Coca-Cola, Walmart, and General Motors are examples of this firm type.

Big Data Engineer

The Coca-Cola Company • Atlanta, GA, US

This job is no longer accepting applications

1 connection works here

Job ID: R-22418

Job Description Summary

As a part of Global IT at The Coca-Cola Company we are looking for a Big Data Engineer or Big Data Analyst to join a new team to create business insight on one of the world's most recognizable brands. The Coca-Cola Company sells its products in nearly every country in the world and each year we're adding new products to our portfolio. As you can imagine we have a lot of data and are looking for top talent to help engineer the next generation of data solutions. Some of the tools we use today include Spark, PySpark, Python, Databricks, ETL, SQL, and NoSQL.

We're looking for technologists who understand the fundamentals and principles of data and who want to solve business problems on a global scale in a large, complex environment. We care less about your knowledge of a particular technology or database and care more about your passion, creativity, and aptitude for engineering big data solutions. We also recognize that the tools we use today may not be the tools we use in the future so we are looking for engineers who are adaptable and eager to learn.

Who You Are...

Function Specific Activities:

- Passionate with an aptitude to quickly learn new and emerging technologies

Seniority Level
Entry level

Industry
Consumer Goods, Food Production, Food & Beverages

Employment Type
Full-time

Job Functions
Engineering, Information Technology

Big Data Engineer job profile opening

Multi-Tech Companies Capabilities

Machine learning teams are already well-established in certain large technological organizations. Because they are the ones that pioneered these industries, these are usually huge software corporations. They frequently have large technological teams and some of the world's most talented employees. You'll frequently be working on complex problems that necessitate creative thinking.

This is the place to go if you're looking for a challenge and some of the best training in the world. You'll have access to massive volumes of information. You won't be able to move as quickly as some early-stage startups, but you'll have a decent balance between them and a traditional corporation, with a competitive wage package and, in many cases, a well-known brand on your portfolio when you decide to move on.

Google, Microsoft, Uber, Airbnb, and Facebook are examples of this type of firm.

Minimum qualifications:

- BA/BS degree in Computer Science or related technical field or equivalent practical experience.
- 2 years of work or educational experience in Machine Learning or Artificial Intelligence.
- 1 year of relevant work experience, including software development.
- Experience with one or more general purpose programming languages including but not limited to: Java, C/C++ or Python.

Preferred qualifications:

- MS or PhD degree in Computer Science, Artificial Intelligence, Machine Learning, or related technical field.
- Experience with one or more of the following: Natural Language Processing, text understanding, classification, pattern recognition, recommendation systems, targeting systems, ranking systems or similar.

Desired qualifications and requirements in different machine learning openings

Data Scientist - Strategic Analytics, Experiences

Airbnb • San Francisco, CA, US

This job is no longer accepting applications

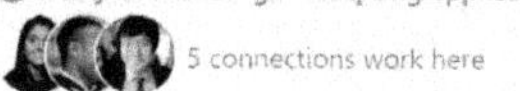

5 connections work here

Airbnb Experiences are handcrafted activities designed and led by local experts. We launched Experiences in November 2016 with the ambitious goal of taking Airbnb from an accommodations business to an end to end travel platform. Since then, the Experiences team has been growing the new product exponentially, helping our hosts build new businesses and our guests experience travel in completely new ways. In the past year, we've seen a wide variety of Experiences succeed, everything from cooking in the Tuscany Countryside to flying a plane over Los Angeles to a Wolf Encounter.

The Data Science team plays a crucial role in realizing this mission by understanding our users and fueling actionable data insights to drive huge impact in a wide range of areas from influencing business strategies, product direction to operational excellence. As the Data Scientist- Strategic Analytics, you'll have the potential for massive impact, influencing key strategic decisions by bringing data to the table when it matters most.

Responsibilities

- Recommend business strategy using deep understanding of data & what drives growth for our business
- Drive impact through compelling data backed recommendations to executives
- Frame & communicate your recommendations with a clear view into the assumptions you have made and the rigor employed in the analysis
- Investigate questions around user experience to understand the voice of our users at scale
- Leverage Airbnb's rich data and state-of-art data science

Industry
Hospitality, Internet, Leisure, Travel & Tourism

Employment Type
Full-time

Job Functions
Research, Science, Engineering

Data Scientist job profile opening

Ways to Look Into Data Science Companies

Identifying the quality of the organization you want to join is one of the most significant components of acquiring a decent job in machine learning and AI.

Examine DS Approach

From a technological standpoint, think about the problems the company is trying to solve, its methodology, its data, how it audits and monitors itself, and whether it is using machine learning sensibly.

I've included these powerful guiding questions completely from Karen Hao's recent post in the MIT Technology Review since they are so spot-on:

1. What issue is it attempting to address? Is the company's stated goal deserving of machine learning? Perhaps we're speaking with Affectiva, a company that develops emotion recognition software that can correctly track and evaluate people's moods. This is a pattern identification problem, thus machine learning could help (see What is Machine Learning?). It would also be difficult to tackle it in a different way because it is far too complex to put into a set of rules.
2. How is the business using machine learning to solve this problem? We want to hear how the company plans to address the issue now that we have a conceptual understanding of it. A company that specializes in emotion recognition could create its product in a variety of ways. It could teach a computer vision system to recognize patterns in people's faces, or an audio system to recognize patterns in people's voice tones. We're trying to find out how the corporation turned its problem into a machine-learning challenge and what data it'll need to feed into its algorithms.
3. Where does the firm get its training data? We want to know how the organization acquires the data after we know what kind of data it requires. Most AI applications rely on supervised machine learning, which necessitates the usage of clean, well-labeled data. Who is responsible for data labeling? Do the labels follow a scientific standard if the labels are subjective, such as emotions? In the instance of Affectiva, you'd find that the corporation collects audio and video data from consumers freely, then hires trained professionals to classify the data in a strict, consistent manner. Knowing the specifics of this section of the pipeline can also help you spot any sources of data collecting or labeling bias.
4. Is there a system in place for auditing the company's products? We should now look into whether or not the corporation tests its products. What is the accuracy of its algorithms? Are they subjected to a bias investigation? How frequently does it re-evaluate its algorithms to ensure that they are still operating well? What plans does the

organization have in place if it doesn't yet have algorithms that achieve the required accuracy or fairness before deploying them?

5. Is it appropriate for the corporation to use machine learning to solve this issue? This is a more subjective decision. Even if machine learning can fix an issue, it's crucial to consider whether it should. Just because you can build an emotion identification platform that can recognize emotions with at least 80% accuracy across races and genders doesn't imply it won't be exploited. Do the advantages of having this technology outweigh the possibility for emotional surveillance to violate human rights? Is there any system in place to offset any potential negative consequences?

A company with a high-quality machine learning product, in my opinion, should be tackling a problem that is well-suited to machine learning, have a robust data acquisition pipeline and auditing processes, have high-accuracy algorithms, or a plan to improve them, and be confronting ethical issues head-on. Frequently, businesses pass the first four exams but fail the final one. That raises a significant red flag for me. It shows that the corporation isn't thinking about how its technology may affect people's lives holistically, and it has a good possibility of pulling a Facebook later.

So, utilize Karen Hao's amazing five-question approach to determine whether a company's machine learning product is on the right road.

An even shorter, no-nonsense list from a startup buddy of mine is as follows:

- Leadership that is capable and transparent.
- People with a lot of energy, both good and bad.
- Early on in the process, perhaps the first official product or engineering hire.
- Product-market fit has been confirmed, but there is still a lot of product development to be done.
- Difficult difficulties that will keep you up at night.
- Addressing a real and pressing need

Put your most crucial criteria first, and don't settle for anything less.

Examine the Company Culture

People talk about culture all the time, and how crucial fit is for both candidates and companies.

My final tip is to do this during the interview process, particularly during the behavioral sections. There's nothing like spending time with a company in person to understand more about how it works. However, there are a few basic techniques to "screen" a firm to learn more about its culture and employees.

1. Take a look at Glassdoor. It's undoubtedly the best online collection of corporate information, with reviews from both current and former employees as well as people who have interviewed with the company. It's fairly simple: if there are a lot of negative reviews, you should probably avoid it. As a result, it's a fantastic, rapid way to assess a company's reputation. The Glassdoor approach, on the other hand, might be challenging, especially when dealing with a very small or very large organization. It's possible that there won't be any reviews at all for the former. However, with such a vast organization, it's possible that none of the reviews are related to the machine learning division.
2. Check out the most recent company news. One of the simplest methods to do this is to visit the company's website and look through their online press room to see what they've recently published. However, that is only the company's approved public relations. You should also conduct some basic Google searches. Obviously, if they've lately received negative press, you should conduct further due diligence on the company.
3. Use LinkedIn to find out more. Examine present personnel, including those you'll be working with directly and those at the director level and above. You should look into their past to see what schools they attended, what hobbies they participate in, and, of course, their most recent employment history and how they define their job. If you notice certain commonalities and items that pique your interest, it's possible that the company is a good match for you. It's also worth noting that other organizations simply hire in a different way. Some companies, for example, are seeking specialists rather than generalists. Some are seeking applicants who are completely formed, while others are looking for persons who can be trained. Looking through existing employee profiles can help you get a sense of what that organization likes, and then you can decide whether that is something you want to do.

Now that you've done some research on firms, let's look into landing an interview.

CHAPTER THREE

How to Get into a Job Interview

Even more than getting through the interview, having an interview is sometimes the most difficult element of getting the job. As a result, in this section, we'll show you how to get an interview in the first place.

I divided the section into traditional and proactive techniques, both of which can help you stand out in a crowd of contenders, especially at startups.

Roadmaps to Get into an Interview

The majority of organizations have a career portal where they list job openings. You can always use that jobs portal to target a company and react to a specific job advertisement or to submit a general application indicating broader interest in the company. Job advertisements for machine learning can also be found on sites like Indeed and LinkedIn. These are old standbys. Invest some time there without a doubt.

Recruiters

You'll normally work with a recruiter during the interview process, but you don't have to wait for them to contact you. You have the option of directly contacting recruiters, either within the company (in-house recruiter) or through third-party recruiters who connect companies with great candidates.

Recruiters specializing in artificial intelligence and machine learning are available. They may use a more broad word like "technical recruiter" or mention this in their LinkedIn profile title. Recruiters are essential because they may be aware of openings that aren't even publicized on the internet. Keep in mind that about half of the positions aren't even listed. A short search on LinkedIn can turn up a number of local recruiters who could be able to put you in touch with the right companies.

Recruitment Drive

Job fairs can be intimidating: who wants to be mingling with a slew of other hopefuls while attempting to track down corporate representatives at a booth? However, career fairs at prominent institutions, in particular, can be quite good. However, networking activities and meetups within your local machine learning community are likely to be more beneficial than a standard job fair.

Quick Interview

While the methods listed above are fairly standard, it's becoming increasingly usual for candidates to take a different approach to land a job interview. In order to secure a job, you'll often have to hustle and show your inventiveness and tenacity. Startups are known for pioneering a novel form of interview technique, and they are one of the key sectors of new jobs in AI and machine learning.

Participate or Plan an Event

This is frequently the best method to meet people in your community who are interested in AI and machine learning, and you might hear about career prospects from the attendees. Depending on what you're searching for, you can attend huge conferences or smaller, more targeted community events.

Seminars/Webinars/Conferences

International Conference on Machine Learning (ICML)

With more than 35 years in the business, ICML is one of the world's premier international machine learning conferences. It's usually held in California and has a panel of experts who discuss the present state and future of machine learning. If you're a machine learning engineer, this event is a must-attend, but there's definitely something for everyone involved in the field.

Artificial Intelligence Conference

This conference focuses on the most recent AI and machine learning achievements. It's an O'Reilly event that combines science with business, including speakers from leading software companies, training courses, and opportunities for networking. It's an excellent resource for learning about artificial intelligence's various applications. It's geared toward product managers and business intelligence developers in particular.

Neural Information Processing Systems Conference

This conference, which has been conducted since 1987, focuses on theory and research on the most recent breakthroughs in machine learning. It would be perfect for machine learning researchers or those with a theoretical background because there is a heavy emphasis on computational neuroscience.

Meetups

Attending smaller community gatherings where you may make a stronger impression and potentially take on a leadership role after some time may be more in your interest. It's also a good method to meet new individuals in your neighborhood. Large events are frequently packed with vendors and people looking to form larger collaborations. Small events can help you network with colleagues who can aid you in the future and provide you with better access to hiring managers. You might also be able to secure a speaking engagement or begin to establish a name for yourself in the community.

Meetup.com is one of the greatest places to find meetups. On the site, you'll find a wide variety of them. Some are fairly huge; the NYC Machine Learning Meetup, for example, has over 13,000 members. But don't be put off by this; many individuals will sign up for a Meetup but never show up. A smaller meetup is usually between 10 and 200 participants.

If you can't locate a nice meetup in your area, another option is to start one yourself. I know a lot of job hopefuls who found jobs because they joined a relevant community group. It transforms you into a community connector or influencer. And that's a fantastic position to have on your resume.

Freelance and Build a Portfolio

There's no reason you shouldn't get started with machine learning right away. Freelancing is one of the simplest methods to get started. Designers, engineers, and data scientists will generally have the easiest time with this, but researchers and product managers may also have possibilities. As a qualified professional, sites like Upwork or TopTal make it simple to build a profile and locate employment in short-term contracts, ongoing projects, or even longer-term engagements.

A portfolio can assist you in developing your personal brand while also serving as an online record of your work experience. It can also give you early references and testimonials that you can use to pitch to potential employers. It may also allow you to do some genuinely intriguing work that will motivate you to write articles for blogs or create other content that will help you grow your profile.

Finally, freelancing can help you validate the various forms of employment and industries that interest you, allowing you to narrow your job search and be more specific in the future.

Get Involved in Open Source

Participating in open-source projects is another approach to meeting people in the machine learning community. These are open-source codebases and repositories that are developed by distributed groups and are often not for profit or owned by a corporation. They're frequently found in Github open-source sources. This includes the Natural Language Toolkit project, which aids in the handling of human language as a data source, as well as the Python data science and machine learning toolkit's many libraries.

Companies that hire engineers are recognized for hiring based on open-source contributions, and they may find you based on what you wrote. It works in the same way as the portfolio effect. People will frequently check you up online to see what you've done.

Attend Hackathons

Competition or a hackathon may be the way to go if you wish to employ your skill set in a more confined or time-limited context.

Machine learning competitions, such as Kaggle, and several hackathons, allow you to work swiftly on real-world business or social issues. It's a terrific way to put your machine learning and artificial intelligence talents to work, and you'll have the opportunity to meet new people while also demonstrating your capacity to make a difference.

Interviews follow-ups

The last path in, or step you can take, is a classic, but it can be irreplaceable. Finally, partnerships can set you on the way to a job and assist you in closing the transaction. More than half of all jobs aren't advertised on job boards, and the only way to break through a company's supposedly impenetrable shell is to start meeting people from that organization and developing strong relationships with them.

One of the most effective ways to network is to ask for just a few minutes of someone's time. It's excellent for a short coffee date. Meet them when it's convenient for them, at a location of their choosing. Send an email or a LinkedIn message with a brief message. All you need is one sentence to explain why you're different from other candidates. You may also utilize Steve Blank's excellent framework.

If you get coffee, use it as an opportunity to gather advice and information from others who work in the sector. You'll truly acquire a sense of how the industry works if you're skilled at expanding your network.

CHAPTER FOUR

Profile Building

Use References and Network

Let's take a closer look at networking. A strong referral is one of the most potent sources of information for a company, especially if the referral comes from someone who is already employed there. If you have someone on the inside watching out for you, they'll make sure your application is reviewed, and you may even be able to skip ahead in the interview process.

It's vital to note that these recommendations do not have to be buddies. It could be as simple as remembering a person's name and making a good first impression. They may say something nice like, "Yeah, I met Rob once, he was amazing." That might help you get past the first screen.

The most important thing is to establish relationships before you require them. You should have a long-term approach to this and be on the lookout for fresh opportunities to form and cultivate relationships on a regular basis. When an opportunity presents itself, you'll already have strong contacts or locations to turn for referrals. If you only invest in these relationships when you need help, you won't be as successful. You should also put money into them.

If you find yourself in a situation where you urgently require a referral, you can employ the informational interview strategy. Reaching out to folks in the field to gain a feel of what they're working on is the goal of this strategy. People can be quite giving with their time and volunteer to help you if you approach them in the proper way.

My recommendation is to use social media sites such as LinkedIn and AngelList to find people. Write them a LinkedIn message or get their email address and send them a note once you've found the people you want to chat to.

Here's an example of a template you might want to use:

Hi [name],

I'm fascinated by the difficulties that Google is attempting to solve via machine learning. I've always wanted to work in this subject, and as a dedicated reader of the Think with Google blog, I get monthly updates on how Google is pushing the boundaries of AI and machine learning.

Because of my skills in engineering and design, I may be able to contribute some innovative ideas for assisting Google's current projects.

I'd want to take you out to coffee to learn more about the issues you're dealing with in your position. And maybe I can assist! Do you have any availability in the next weeks?

Cheers,

[your name]

See how far you can get with something like that. One thing to keep in mind is to avoid being discouraged too fast. It could just be a numbers game because people are so busy. Don't take it personally if someone doesn't respond to you.

Checking out your second-degree relationships is one of the most useful LinkedIn features. You might be able to find some mutual ties to bring up with the person you're after.

Do your homework before meeting up with someone for coffee or an informational interview. Do some additional research on the company and the individual you're speaking with. That way, you can ensure that the talk moves smoothly.

Finally, the interview may reveal that you are not interested in working for that organization or on that particular team, which will save you time!

LinkedIn vs. CV

This is a crucial element for you, especially if you come from an academic background. People aren't always interested in reading your CV when you're seeking for work. If you're applying for a highly focused research position, you'll need to offer yourself in a more comprehensible format, which you can do through LinkedIn. LinkedIn is a gold standard for recruitment, even if you have an amazing CV. Potential employers and recruiters will be able to find you, evaluate you, and possibly get you a job if you have a well-designed and clear LinkedIn profile.

LinkedIn is used by everyone. You may already be losing out to other prospects if you don't stand out on LinkedIn. Resumes are frequently thought to be overrated, but LinkedIn profiles, in my opinion, are not. It's more than a resume of your achievements. It should tell a story, and leveraging your LinkedIn profile for a variety of purposes can help you stand out.

As a result of the information and comments they provide on LinkedIn on a daily basis, several people I know have received job and speaking offers. One of my strategies is to follow people in my industry who are influential, comment on their posts, and appreciate their work. Send them a message on purpose after you've established a presence through these meetings.

Those with an academic background place a high value on publication. However, when applying for these types of jobs, it's critical to be succinct and talk about the impact and metrics you've achieved. Because recruiters will peruse them quickly, you'll want to be as concise as possible. Use keywords that are specific to your industry. Make sense of the numbers you're using. Also, don't underestimate your own worth.

Resume Generation

It's unlikely that the method you were taught to do something in school is the best way to accomplish it. It's also crucial, particularly for small firms and promising startups. They want to know about you as a person and how you'll fit into the corporate culture.

In your email to the recruiting manager, include a few key paragraphs or bullet points about your experiences and interests. Maintain succinctness, brevity, and personalization. Explain why your experience might be valuable to their business and what you hope to learn from it. It's possible that's all you'll need.

A more extensive approach with some great examples of how to enhance a cover letter can be found here.

Interview Preparation

Once you've landed an interview, you'll be invited to start the process, which normally involves a screening call with a recruiter. In this section, I'll go over the typical interview process for AI and machine learning jobs.

Expectation

In the machine learning sector, an interview often includes behavioral questions with a variety of difficult technical questions. It's crucial to note that every organization is different, and the hiring processes for various roles may differ significantly. Some businesses will wish to concentrate on in-depth, highly technical issues. Others will place a greater emphasis on cultural fit and behavioral issues. Because you're likely to have a combination of both, it's a good idea to plan ahead of time and holistically.

One of the firms we'll discuss later, Integrate.ai, for example, places a strong emphasis on the behavioral interview, and even if a candidate has the finest technical interview, they won't be considered if they aren't a cultural match. The following is an example of a normal and thorough procedure:

Phone screens are used to eliminate candidates who do not meet the job's basic requirements. They also serve to verify whether a candidate's claimed experience is true.

The interview will most likely be conducted by someone from human resources rather than the recruiting manager to save time. These interviews are typically used to assess if you fit into a company's culture and how you collaborate with others. It's also a great opportunity to show off your communication skills.

Throughout the conversation, you'll be asked questions, but you'll also want to ask your own, such as:

- What kinds of issues does the machine learning team have to deal with?
- What are the company's main objectives?
- What are the company's core values?
- To whom would I be reporting?
- Are you able to provide a salary range for this position?
- If I were to go ahead with the interview, how would it go?
- How should I best prepare for the next level if I decide to continue forward?

Also, think about other intelligent questions that can help you better understand their business, the environment in which they operate, and the role itself.

Assessments

Companies will typically offer you a project and a deadline after a phone interview, which is normally a few days or a week. Companies often utilize a second screening stage to ensure that you have a minimum degree of technical abilities and understanding, as well as some reasoning power and problem-solving aptitude, for the work. It also eliminates people who have difficulty with commitment.

So, what kinds of tasks can you do at home? It could be anything from a detailed examination of a specific data set to dissecting a machine learning system to show your understanding. It could also be a coding project for the development of an app. Finding out what kind of challenges you're dealing with should be one of your goals in this method.

The most important thing to remember is that most interviews focus on your approach and problem-solving skills rather than the results or whether you got the right answers. If you demonstrate some level of inventiveness and problem-solving aptitude, it's often acceptable to fail. If you have a lot of coding to do, write it down clearly and thoroughly so that an interviewer can follow your thought processes and comprehend what you did.

According to a KDNuggets post, you should:

1. Make an ML template that includes reusable functions.
2. Create an API based on SciKit-Learn and Matplotlib that allows you to do EDA and construct simple models easily.
3. To raise the eyebrows of an interviewer, consider layering different models or employing one model prediction in another.

Consider reading the blogs of key firms like Google, Facebook, Twitter, and others for case studies, since you may often get a better feel of how these companies use machine learning to solve business problems.

You'll usually be given a deadline for take-home tasks; for example, it could take 5-6 hours and you'll have to turn it in within a couple of days. Of course, the goal is to stay within those boundaries while remaining truthful. Go as far as you can, and if you find yourself straying beyond the intended limitations, make a list of what you would do if you had more time to work on the problem.

Conversation with Manager

If you make it beyond the initial couple of screens—which some say can eliminate up to half of all applicants—you'll almost certainly be scheduled for a meeting with the hiring manager (i.e., the person who is actually hiring you).

This interview will most likely focus on your technical abilities, and it will most likely be the final screen and phone conversation before you arrive on-site. This is normally separated into two or three parts, which are usually done over one long phone call but can also be done over three shorter phone calls of 30 minutes each.

Hands-On

This is the most usual component of the interview, especially for a machine learning engineer. You'll most likely be judged on your ability to tackle a coding challenge by presenting pseudocode or compile-ready code in more difficult interviews. If you're looking for a data position, you'll almost certainly be asked how to query data using SQL. The questions you'll be asked will most likely be in the programming scripting languages you indicated you're familiar with Python, Java, Ruby, or whatever language you use.

Your interviewer may use online whiteboarding software or ask you to share your screen to evaluate you online. They can even request that you collaborate with them in a text editor and type in your response. Practice using programs like HackerRank or Collabedit to prepare for these scenarios.

There are numerous online resources for coding interviews, ranging from Cracking the Coding Interview to Interview Cake. Use them to your advantage.

Statistical Analysis

It's possible that you'll receive a call that checks for essential mathematics and statistical concepts. This is especially true for people seeking data science positions. Your knowledge of A/B split testing, how p-values are determined, and what statistical significance implies will likely be prioritized by web companies. Regression in linear algebra may be used more frequently by energy businesses. In any of these interviews, the most important thing to remember is to reveal your full thought process.

If they inquire about A/B tests, for example, explain the process in detail, emphasize what to avoid, and share your own experiences. Show off your statistical reasoning skills by treating these puzzles as though they were mathematical proofs. Also, don't be hesitant to share a story about why this is important and what insights you might be able to provide as a consequence with a corporation.

Talk over Recent Trends

The hiring manager's final question will be about how you communicate and whether you'll fit in with the rest of the team. The purpose of this conversation is for the hiring manager to gain a sense of who you are, including your character, motivations, fit with the team, and intelligence. The idea is to show who you are and why you're the best candidate for the job not just because of your talents, but also because of your personality and characteristics.

As you prepare for this round of the interview, think about the challenges the hiring manager is facing and the type of person they're looking for. They may already have an image of the person's traits in their heads. Although you are not striving to be a chameleon, you can change the tone of your conversation by emphasizing essential aspects of your personality. Another thing to think about is if you'd pass "the airplane test. "Would you like to spend several hours on an airplane with someone you don't know?

Interview Analysis

It's time to meet your recruiting manager in person if you've made it this far. They'll assess you both technically and non-technically. This will go over your qualifications as a candidate in further detail.

The action picks up on-site as well. I've put together a list of questions that you can use in this interview or the sections that follow.

Challenge

If you don't face a technical obstacle during your first on-site interview, you'll almost certainly face one during your second, especially if you're interviewing for an engineering position. You can be asked to write down how you would implement particular algorithms or approach specific business problems on a whiteboard.

This necessitates brushing up on your technical abilities and knowledge of crucial phrases. You're unlikely to get the job if you don't succeed or at least demonstrate potential in the technical component of the on-site interview.

Recruiting Manager

If you get through a pair of interviews with the recruiting manager, you're almost done with the process, and you'll most likely meet members of the executive team at that time. If it's a startup, this may even be the founder and/or CEO.

Congratulations if you've made it this far. It usually means you've already "passed" the other portions and it's time to narrow down your options and select the best candidates. The goal is to show why you are the best applicant for the position. In general, keep doing what you're doing, and don't let anxiety get in the way.

In most cases, the executive interview will not be technical. Most likely, it's about confirming their pick based on fit and how well you align with the company's strategic strategy. It's also an excellent time to talk about how you see yourself progressing with the company, rather than just how you'd fit into a specific function.

CHAPTER FIVE

Interview Preparation

I've broken it down into two major categories: behavioral and technical. I've also broken down the technical section into sub-categories (e.g., algorithms, probability, and more).

One suggestion I've received is to read the full fifth chapter of the MIT Press "Deep Learning" book, which covers machine learning fundamentals. It's available for free here.

I've done my best to compile tactical examples, proofs, and resources that you may apply directly to verified questions in machine learning interviews.

These questions are used to evaluate an applicant's qualitative skills and fit, including past work situations and scenarios, as well as teamwork skills.

Previous Work

Can you tell me about a previous AI/machine learning project you worked on?

The goal of the question is to get a sense of your breadth of knowledge and contributions from previous experiences. It assesses your ability to create a story about your work and tie it to the impact you have on the firm.

Answering questions

- Make an effort to describe a project that exhibits both product and engineering knowledge. If you discovered a machine learning model that may solve a business problem, for example, you should describe how these themes contributed to the company's growth.

- Explain your contribution and the outcome in terms of the company's goals. While trying to comprehend the overarching purpose of the project, the interviewer wants to know what you did particularly.
- As much as possible, rehearse your experiences. Because this is a common topic, come up with two or three projects that you can discuss in depth.

previous job satisfaction

The purpose of the inquiry is to determine whether the position you're applying for is a good fit for you and why you're leaving a previous job.

Response to the questions

- You should have a good understanding of the function. If feasible, use your HR contact to learn as much as possible about the role and its problems before the interview. HR can be a gold mine of information about the function, team, history, and urgent company objectives.
- avoid discussing personal concerns with individual people, and when sharing your dislikes, maintain a professional demeanor. Examine your motivations and examine yourself carefully. For example, as a fun activity, talk about how to solve a machine learning difficulty in a practical approach. You might also talk about how to master new technologies that enable machine learning to be deployed across a company. You can object to the company's inability to priorities AI/ML in its strategy, or to the fact that the company's management has experienced significant turnover, leaving the team's direction in doubt. Maintain a positive attitude and avoid discussing personal concerns.
- Bad: "I didn't appreciate how management had no idea where the firm was going!"
- Good: "I realized I wanted to work for a company that uses AI and machine learning as part of its fundamental strategy and has a clear vision."

Situational

Tell me about a time when you needed to persuade others to agree with you on something. What was the outcome?

The goal is to see how proficient you are at defending your position and how adaptable you are as part of a team.

How to respond to the question: Think of a time when you were effective in making a change, and then talk about how the change was quantifiable in its effects. Use a machine learning or AI example if possible. You must exhibit your ability to communicate and lead in this situation.

I frequently employ a framework developed by the prominent business consulting firm McKinsey to describe circumstances and outcomes:

Situation-Complication-Resolution is a three-part framework.

- The framing of a significant, recent context that the audience is already familiar with and accepts as fact.
- The reason the issue necessitates action is because of the complication.
- Resolution is the action required to address a problem (or capture an opportunity).

The bottom line is that you should describe a situation that was going along normally, a trigger event or problem that threw everything off, and how you pushed the team to resolve it. This will demonstrate that you don't only respond instinctively, but that you consider solutions to difficulties.

Please keep in mind that this is a generic framework that can be used in a wide range of circumstances.

In general, the workflow of ML projects

This is one of the most useful frameworks I've seen for approaching a machine learning project in general. It's as follows:

- Define your company's goal. Are we attempting to get more customers, increase satisfaction, or increase revenue?
- Define the problem. What is the exact gap that machine learning can close between your ideal world and reality? Create a list of questions that your data and predictive modeling can help you solve (ML algorithms).
- Make a common-sense starting point. Set up a baseline to answer the problem as if you know nothing about data science before resorting to machine learning. You may be surprised by how effective this baseline

is. It might be as easy as proposing the top N most popular goods, or it could be more complicated. This baseline can also be used to measure the performance of machine learning algorithms.

- Examine the ML literature. To avoid recreating the wheel and to gather ideas on what techniques/algorithms are most effective at answering the questions using our data.
- Create a single-digit metric. What does success imply (high accuracy, lower error, or a larger AUC)? And how are you going to measure it? The metric must be in line with high-level objectives. Set a single metric against which all models will be judged.
- Analyze data in an exploratory manner. Play around with the data to gain a sense of the many sorts of data, their distribution, variable correlation, aspects, and so on. This stage would necessitate a great deal of plotting.
- Partitioning of data. The validation set should be large enough to find differences between the models you're training; the test set should be large enough to demonstrate the final model's overall performance; and, of course, the training set should be large enough to show the final model's overall performance.
- Preprocess. Data integration, cleaning, transformation, reduction, discretization, and other operations fall under this category.
- Invent characteristics. It's challenging, time-consuming, and requires specialist knowledge to come up with features. Feature engineering is what applied machine learning is all about. Using domain knowledge, this process usually entails feature selection and creation. For deep learning tasks, it can be kept to a bare minimum.
- Create models. Select an algorithm to employ, hyper-parameters to tweak, architecture to use, and so on.
- Ensemble. Depending on the correlations of the models/features, ensemble approaches can usually improve performance. As a result, experimenting is always a smart idea. However, be willing to make tradeoffs—some ensemble approaches are too complex/slow to implement in production.
- Models should be deployed. Models should be deployed in production for inference.
- Keep an eye on the models. Keep an eye on the model's performance and solicit feedback.
- Repetition of the preceding steps is required. Data science is a process that is iterated over time, with new and improved models being

generated.

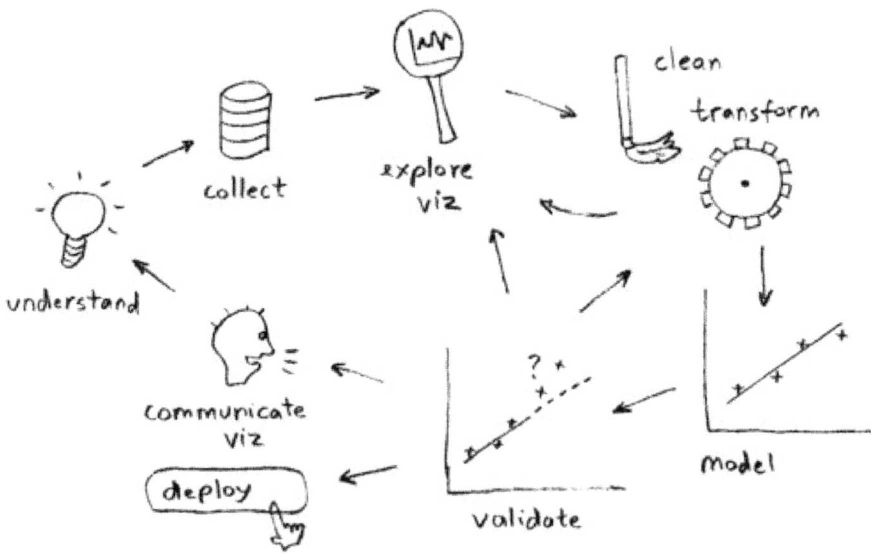

Basic understanding of responses to the hiring manager

Technical Interview Questions

In a machine learning interview, you may be asked a variety of technical questions, which will differ depending on the function and the company. Algorithms and theory, maths and probability, programming skills and the application of theory to code, and finally your broad understanding of AI and machine learning could all be discussed during your interview. It's vital to keep up with the current developments in the sector because it moves so quickly. There will almost certainly be company- or industry-specific questions that will test your ability to translate your general knowledge into useful business insights.

Note: I've taken the liberty of directly quoting questions and solutions from a variety of sources, and I've tried to include attribution and links whenever possible. To keep it simple, I don't include quotations. This is a collection of other people's good work, and I've compiled the best and most simple solutions I could find.

Statistical Analysis

Linear Algebra

What are the differences between scalars, vectors, matrices, and tensors?

The vector and the matrix are the two most important mathematical entities in linear algebra. They are examples of a tensor, which is a broader concept. The number of dimensions in an array required to represent a tensor is determined by its order (or rank). A 0th-order tensor is made up of single integers, which are called scalars. Vectors are 1st-order tensors that are ordered arrays of single numbers. Vectors are members of vector spaces, which are objects. Matrices are rectangular arrays of numbers that are a type of second-order tensor.

The Hadamard product of two matrices is what?

Components from the same row and column of two vectors/matrices are multiplied to form a new vector/matrix in the Hadamard product of two vectors, which is analogous to matrix addition.

$$\vec{g} \circ \vec{h} \circ \vec{m}$$

Vectors g, h, and m Hadamard product.

The order of the matrices to be multiplied must match, and the output matrix must match as well.

$$\overset{G}{\begin{bmatrix} 3 & 5 & 7 \\ 4 & 9 & 8 \end{bmatrix}} \circ \overset{H}{\begin{bmatrix} 1 & 6 & 3 \\ 0 & 2 & 9 \end{bmatrix}} = \overset{N}{\begin{bmatrix} 3\times1 & 5\times6 & 7\times3 \\ 4\times0 & 9\times2 & 8\times9 \end{bmatrix}}$$

Matrix N is the Hadamard product of Matrix G and Matrix H (both of order 2x3).

$$N$$
$$\begin{bmatrix} 3 & 30 & 21 \\ 0 & 18 & 72 \end{bmatrix}$$

The order of N matrices is the same as the order of the input matrices (2x3). JPEG and other picture compression algorithms use the Hadamard product.

What does broadcasting have to do with linear algebra?

NumPy's mechanism for allowing array arithmetic between arrays of different shapes or sizes is known as broadcasting. Although it was first developed for NumPy, the method is now widely utilized in other numerical computing libraries such as Theano, TensorFlow, and Octave.

By effectively reproducing the smaller array along the last mismatched dimension, broadcasting overcomes the problem of arithmetic between arrays of various shapes. Numpy's treatment of arrays of diverse forms during arithmetic operations is referred to as broadcasting. The smaller array is "broadcast" across the bigger array, subject to specific limits so that their shapes are consistent.

NumPy does not copy the smaller array; instead, it makes efficient use of existing memory structures to achieve the same result. The idea has also infiltrated linear algebra notation, making it easier to explain elementary operations.

We also employ some non-traditional notation in the area of deep learning. We can combine a matrix and a vector to get a new matrix: C = A + b, where Ci,j = Ai,j + bj. To put it another way, the vector b is multiplied by each row of the matrix. Before doing the addition, this shorthand eliminates the requirement to build a matrix with b copied into each row. Broadcasting refers to the implied copying of b to several sites.

Linear and Logistic Regression

What is the difference between linear and logistic regression?

For ML algorithms, linear and logistic regression are typically utilized. In an interview, you should expect to be asked at least one of these questions.

The link between the dependent variable Y and the independent variable X is modeled using linear regression.

A binary dependent variable is modeled using logistic regression. Analyze a set of data and come up with a model that can predict this response variable.

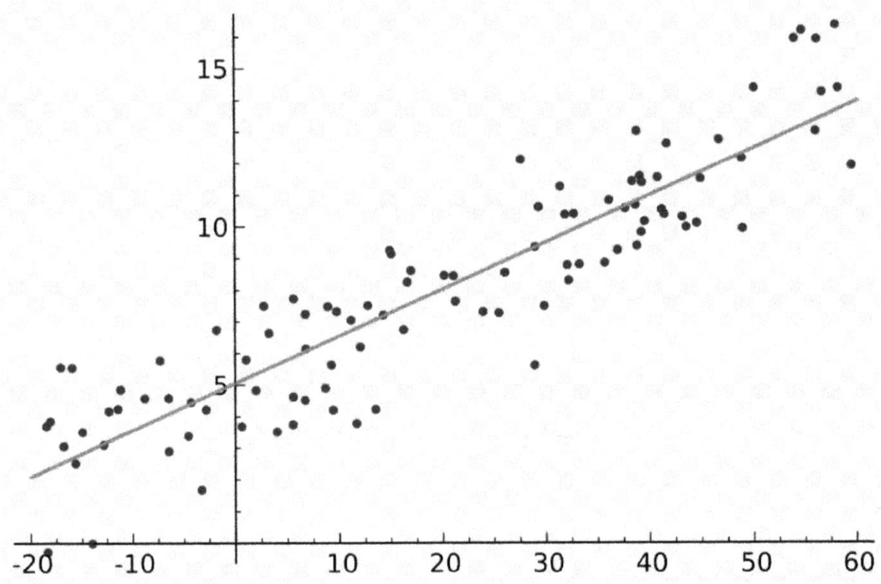

One pen costs x dollars. The cost of ten pens is ten dollars. This is the most common type of linear regression used by laypeople. The simplest version of the regression equation with one dependent and one independent variable is y = c + b*x, where y represents the estimated dependent variable score, c represents the constant, b represents the regression coefficient, and x represents the independent variable score. In our pen example, c=0, y represents the pen cost, and x represents the number of pens. We can compute the cost of any number of pens if we know the unit cost of one pen b. To anticipate house prices, a complicated type of linear regression is applied.

It's easy to make the error of starting with a complicated ML algorithm for every scenario-based challenge in an interview. The majority of interviewees make the mistake of beginning with something that resembles the problem. They could begin by using neural networks or SVMs. If at all possible, begin with linear/logistic regression. This allows you to level-set on the solution's most basic benchmark performance. Approach the question in the same way you would a programming interview, starting with a benchmark and working your way up to a more optimal answer.

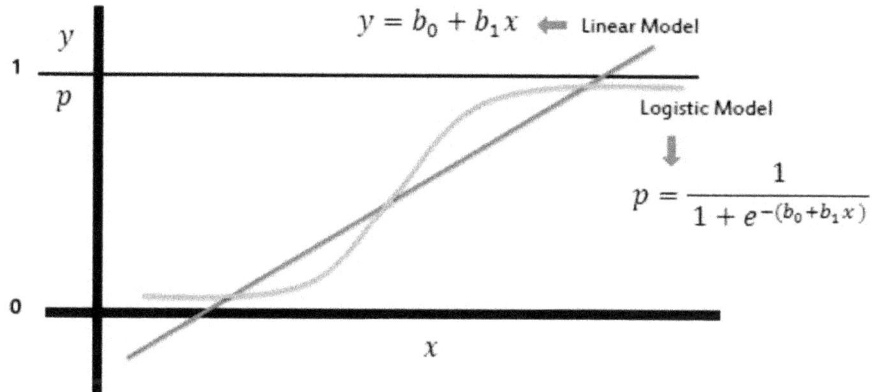

Logistic Model

For continuous goals, linear regression is employed, whereas for binary targets, logistic regression is utilized, as the sigmoid curve in the logistic model drives the characteristics to either a 0 or a 1.

Support Vector Machine

Logistic regression vs. SVMs: When to use which one?

The SVM algorithm seeks to maximize the margin between the closest support vectors, whereas the LR algorithm tries to maximize the posterior class probability. As a result, SVM produces a solution that is as fair as possible for the two categories, whereas LR does not.

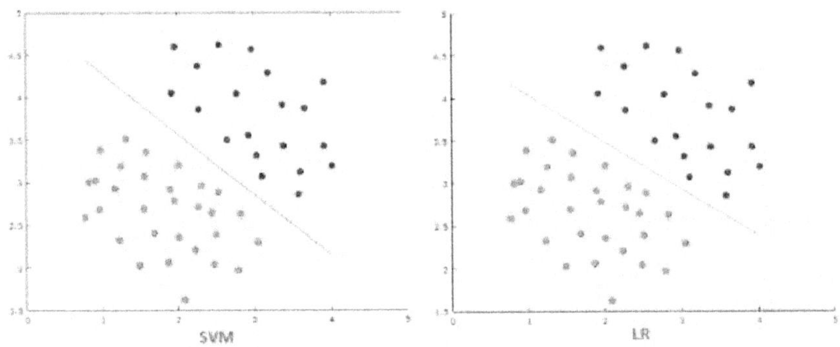

SVM generalization

Because it is easier, start with logistic regression. If logistic regression fails and you suspect your data will not be linearly separable, consider an SVM with a non-linear kernel, such as a Radial Basis Function (RBF).

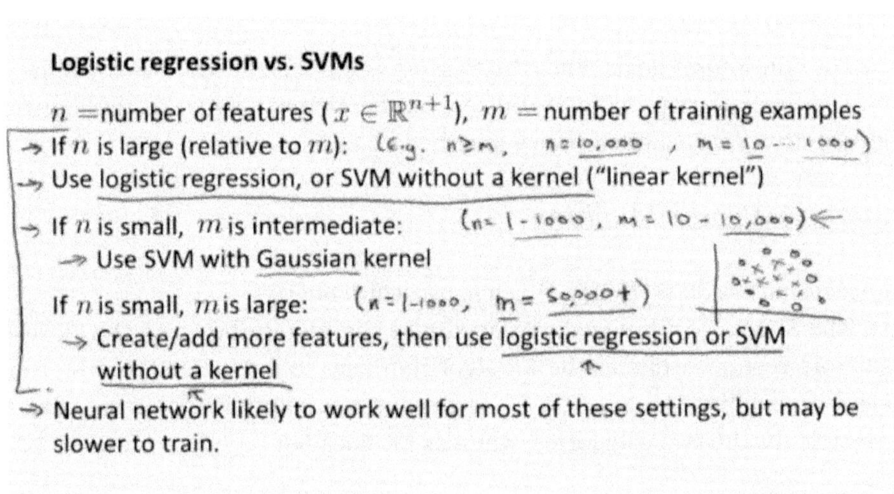

What is the best way to get the SVM optimization function from the logistic regression optimization function? What is a classifier with a large margin?

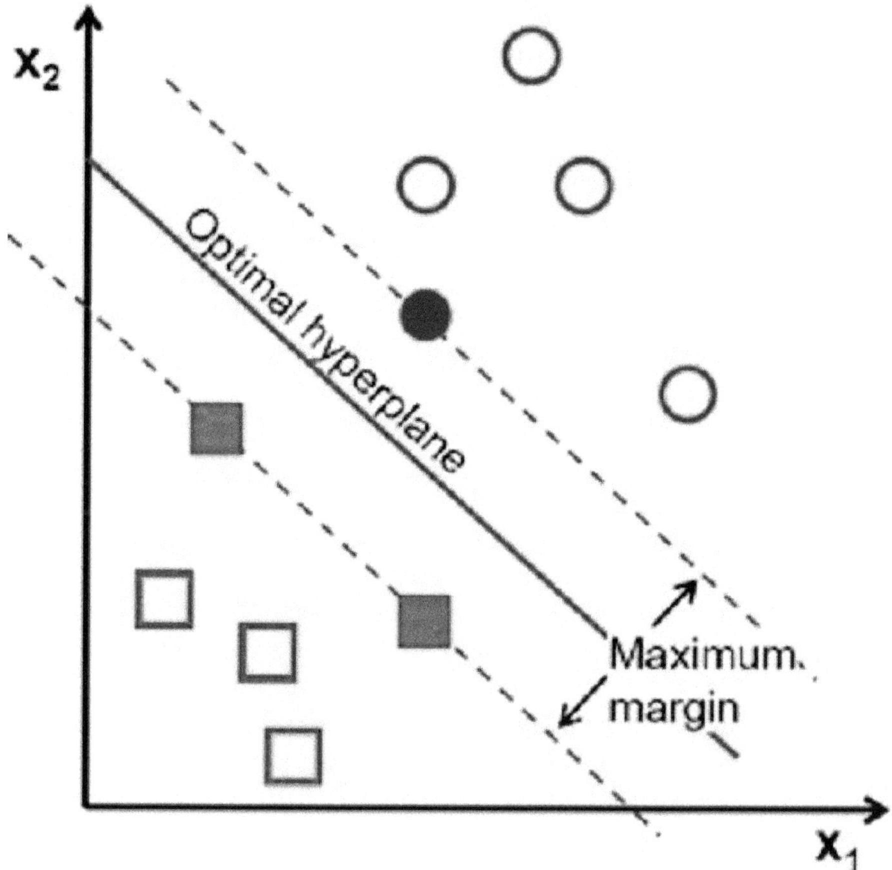

SVM optimization

- SVM is a form of a classifier that distinguishes between positive and negative examples, such as blue and red data points in this case.
- To avoid overfitting, the biggest margin is found, as illustrated in the image. That is, the ideal hyperplane is as far away from the positive and negative instances as possible (equally distant from the boundary lines).
- The margin is maximized to satisfy this requirement, as well as to accurately categories the data points, which is why this is known as the large margin classifier.

Numerical Optimization

What is Ordinary Least Square and Maximum Likelihood?

To linear regression, OLS stands for ordinary least squares. Logistic regression uses maximum likelihood. Explain what the statement means.

The approaches employed by the separate regression methods to approximate the unknown parameter (coefficient) value are OLS and maximum likelihood. Ordinary least squares is a linear regression approach that approximates the parameters, resulting in the shortest gap between actual and predicted values. Maximum likelihood aids in the selection of parameter values that maximize the possibility that the parameters will produce observed data.

Maximum Likelihood

What is the difference between underflow and overflow?

When the absolute value of a number surpasses the computer's ability to represent it, overflow occurs. Underflow occurs when a number's absolute value is too close to 0 for the computer to represent.

Integers and floating-point numbers both have the potential for overflow. Underflow is only possible with floating-point numbers. Multiply a number by 10 repeatedly to generate an overflow. Divide it by ten over and over to produce an underflow.

If the variable x is a signed byte, then its values can range from -239 to +238.

1. x = 239
2. An overflow will occur if x = x + 1. +239 is not a valid value for x

The range of floating-point numbers is determined by their representation. If x is a 32-bit IEEE single-precision number, then

1. x = 1e-38
2. An underflow will occur if x = x / 1000 is used. For x, 1e-42 is not a valid value.

Statistics & Probability

What is Bayes‘ Theorem, and how does it work? What role does it play in machine learning?

Given prior knowledge, Bayes’ Theorem calculates the posterior probability of an event. It’s calculated as the true positive rate of a condition sample divided by the sum of the population’s false positive rate and the condition’s true positive rate. Assume you had a 60% risk of having the flu following a flu test, but the test will be false 50% of the time among those who had the flu, and the whole population has just a 5% chance of having the flu. Would you have a 60% risk of getting the flu if you had a positive test?

No, according to Bayes‘ Theorem. It states you have a 5.94 percent risk of catching the flu if you have a (.6 * 0.05) (True Positive Rate of a Condition Sample) / (.6*0.05) (True Positive Rate of a Condition Sample) + (.5*0.95) (False Positive Rate of a Population) = 0.0594.

The Naive Bayes classifier is based on Bayes’ Theorem, which is the foundation of a discipline of machine learning. When you’re presented with machine learning interview questions, keep this in mind.

What’s the distinction between a Type I and a Type II error?

A "false positive," or the wrong rejection of the null hypothesis, is referred to as a Type I mistake. A "false negative," or the mistaken acceptance of the null hypothesis, is referred to as a Type II error. So, a Type I error is when you claim something happened when it didn’t, and a Type II error is when you claim nothing is occurring when something is. You could wish to use an example to demonstrate your understanding of the principles and how it relates to the business at hand. A Type I error, often known as a false positive, would be informing a male that he was pregnant, whereas a Type II error would be informing a pregnant woman that she was not.

If you ran a fraud detection company, you might have a high tolerance for false positives (a client won’t care if you send them an email about the possibility of fraud), but a false negative (not detecting fraud when it’s already happening) could be disastrous.

Confidence Intervals

What are the population and sample mean values?

The sample mean is the average of a population-wide random sample. The population means is the average of a group of people.

The sample mean is computed as follows:

Sample Mean $\bar{x} = \frac{1}{n} \sum_{i}^{n} = 1_{a_i}$

where, n = Size of sample

Σ = Add up ai = All the population means can be determined as follows:

Population Mean $\mu = \frac{1}{N} \sum_{i}^{N} = 1_{a_i}$

where N = Size of the population. Σ = Add up ai = All the observations

What is the difference between population and sample standard deviation?

The standard deviation of data distribution is a measurement of its spread. It calculates the standard deviation of the distance between each data point and the mean.

The standard deviation formula we apply depends on whether the data is regarded as a population on its own or a sample representing a larger population.

- We divide by the number of data points, N, if the data is regarded as a population on its own.
- We divide by one less than the number of data points in the sample, n-1 if the data is a sample from a bigger population.

The standard deviation of the population: $\sigma = N\Sigma(xi-\mu)2$

The standard deviation of the sample: $sx = n-1\Sigma(xi-x^{-})2$

The steps in each calculation are identical except for one: when dealing with sample data, we divide by one less than the number of data points.

Variables with a Probability Distribution

What is the definition of a probability distribution?

Probability distributions show the probability of all possible outcomes for a process. It expresses the probability that a single observation of a random variable corresponds to a specific value or range of values. In other words, there is a range of possible values for any random process, as well as a probability that a single pull from the random process would take on one of those values.

What is the definition of a probability mass function?

Probabilities for discrete random variables are calculated using a probability mass function (PMF), also known as a frequency function. Variables from experiments such as dice rolls, picking a number out of a hat, or receiving a high mark on an exam are referred to as "random variables." The word "discrete" refers to the fact that there are only a certain number of possible outcomes. On a die, for example, you can only roll a 1,2,3,4,5, or 6.

The following is an example of a PMF equation: P(X = x)

That simply implies "the likelihood that X takes on the value x".

It's not a particularly useful equation in and of itself; what's more useful is an equation that tells you the likelihood of a specific event occurring. Consider the following scenario: P(X=1) = 0.2 * 0.2.

How you come up with these equations is largely determined by the type of event you're dealing with. The binomial distribution PMF, for example, is:

$$f(x) = \binom{n}{x} p^x (1-p)^{n-x}$$

The Poisson distribution PMF is as follows:

$$\Pr\{Y = k \mid \mu\} = \frac{e^{-\mu}\mu^k}{k!} \qquad \text{for } k = 0, 1, 2, \ldots.$$

What is the definition of a probability density function?

The probability density function is used to express the likelihood of a random variable falling within a specific range of values rather than taking any single value.

You must find P(a x b) to determine the likelihood that X falls within the interval (a, b). An integrable function f(x) satisfying the following conditions is a continuous random variable X with support S:

1. For any x in S, f(x) > 0, indicating that f(x) is positive everywhere in the support S.
2. In the support S, the area under the curve f(x) is 1, which means: $\int Sf(x)dx = 1$

If f(x) is the probability density function of x, then the integral of f(x) across that interval yields the probability that x belongs to A, where A is some interval:

$P(X\in A) = \int Af(x)dx$

Autoencoders

What is an autoencoder, and how does it work? What does it mean when it says "auto-encode"?

The purpose of autoencoders (AEs) is to duplicate their inputs to their outputs. They work by compressing the input into a latent-space representation and reconstructing the output from it.

Data examples are used to automatically train autoencoders. It indicates that it's simple to train specialized instances of the algorithm to perform well on a certain sort of input and that it doesn't involve any additional engineering, only the right training data.

There are two pieces to this type of network:

1. The encoder is the network component that compresses the input into a latent-space representation. The encoding function h=f can be used to represent it (x).
2. Decoder: The goal of this section is to rebuild the input using the latent space representation. A decoding function r=g can be used to represent it (h).

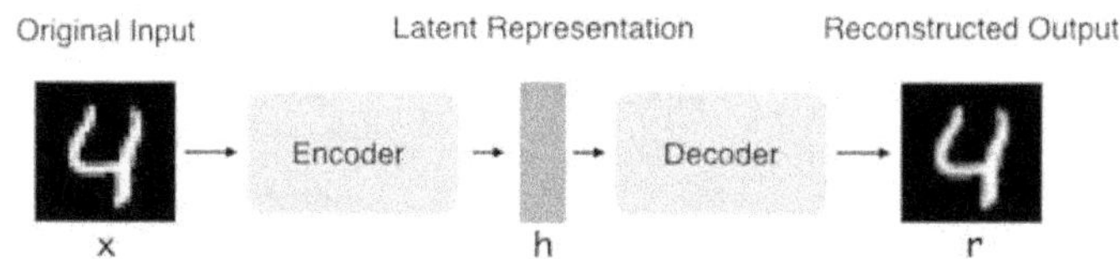

The autoencoder can thus be expressed as a whole by the function g(f(x)) = r, where r should be as near to the original input x as possible.

Programming Skills

Choose an algorithm to implement in parallel and write the pseudocode for it.

This type of inquiry exhibits your parallel thinking skills and your ability to handle concurrency in big data programming methods. To demonstrate your abilities to build parallel programming, check into pseudo-code frameworks like Peril-L and visualization tools like Web Sequence Diagrams.

What are some of the key distinctions between a linked list and an array?

An array is a collection of objects that are arranged in a specific order. A linked list is a collection of objects with pointers indicating how they should be processed in the order. Unlike a linked list, an array believes that each element is the same size. An array must be pre-defined or redefined for organic growth, whereas a linked list can grow naturally. While shuffling a linked list entails changing which points point where shuffling an array is more difficult and requires more memory.

Explain what a hash table is.

A hash table is a data structure that generates a linked list. Through the use of a hash function, a key is translated to specific values. They're frequently utilized for things like database indexing.

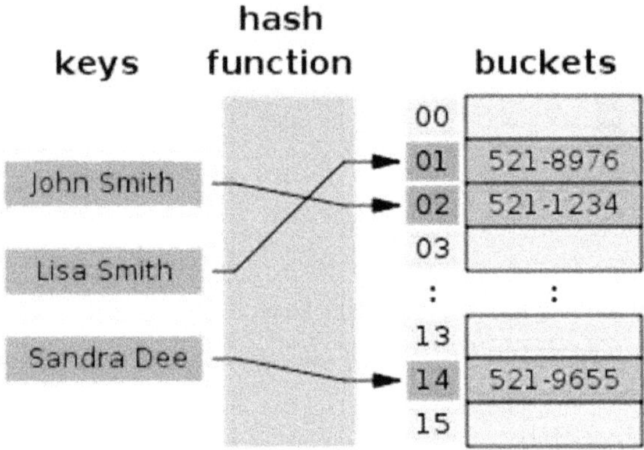

Although most machine learning professions don't require you to be an expert in SQL, a data scientist role is more frequent, and SQL-related difficulties may arise.

Here's a basic rundown of the various types of joins:

- INNER) JOIN: Return records from both tables that have the same values.
- LEFT (OUTER) JOIN: Returns all records from the left table as well as the records from the right table that match.
- RIGHT (OUTER) JOIN: Returns all records from the right table, as well as the records from the left table that are matched.
- FULL (OUTER) JOIN: Return all records when there is a match in either left or right table

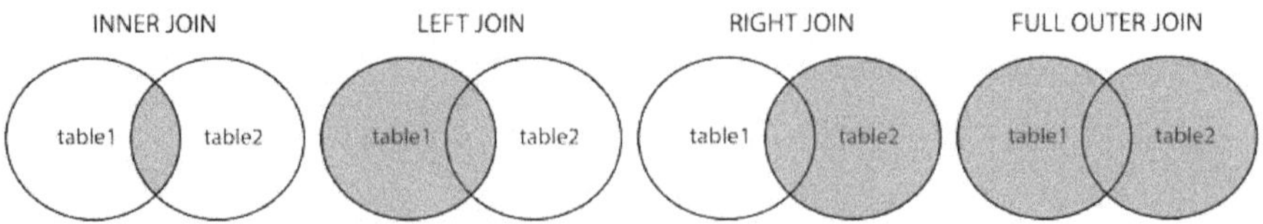

What steps would you take to create a recommendation system for our users?

Many of these types of machine learning interview questions will include applying machine learning models to a company's difficulties. You'll need to do extensive study on the company and its industry, particularly the revenue drivers and the types of users it serves in the context of the sector.

Algorithms and Learning Theory

Bias is an error caused by the learning algorithm's incorrect or excessively simplified assumptions. This can cause the model to underfit your data, making it difficult for it to forecast accurately and for you to transfer your knowledge from the training set to the test set.

Variance is an error caused by a learning method with too much complexity. As a result, the algorithm becomes extremely sensitive to large amounts of variation in your training data, perhaps causing your model to overfit the data. For your model to be useful for your test data, you'll be carrying too much noise from your training data.

The bias-variance decomposition adds bias, variance, and a bit of irreducible error owing to noise in the underlying data set to deconstruct the learning error from any algorithm. In other words, if you make the model more complex and include more variables, you'll lose bias but acquire some variance—you'll have to trade off bias and variance to have the ideally minimized amount of error. You don't want your model to have a lot of bias or variance.

When it comes to machine learning, what's the difference between supervised and unsupervised?

Labeled training data is required for supervised learning. To accomplish classification (a supervised learning task), for example, you must first label the data that will be used to train the model to classify data into your labeled categories. Unsupervised learning, on the other hand, does not necessitate intentional data labeling.

What distinguishes KNN from k-means clustering?

K-means clustering is an unsupervised clustering approach, whereas K-nearest neighbors is a supervised classification algorithm. While the mechanics may appear to be identical at first glance, what this truly means is that you need labeled data to classify an unlabeled point into for k-nearest neighbors to work. Only a collection of unlabeled points and a threshold are required for K-means clustering: the algorithm will accept unlabeled points and eventually learn how to cluster them into groups by computing the mean of the distance between various points.

The key distinction is that KNN requires labeled points and so is supervised learning, but k-means does not and hence is unsupervised learning.

What's your favorite algorithm, and can you tell me about it in under a minute?

This type of question assesses your ability to express difficult and technical details with poise, as well as your ability to summarize information quickly and effectively. Make sure you have an answer and can explain different algorithms in a way that even a five-year-old can understand.

What's a Fourier transform?

A Fourier transform is a method for decomposing generic functions into a superposition of symmetric functions that are used in many applications. It's how we find the recipe if we're handed a smoothie, as this more intuitive lesson puts it. Any temporal signal can be matched using the Fourier transform, which discovers the set of cycle speeds, amplitudes, and phases that correspond to it. A Fourier transform transforms a signal from the time domain to the frequency domain, and it's a popular method for extracting features from audio signals or other time series like sensor data.

Data Sets and Big Data

On a time series data set, what cross-validation approach would you use?

Instead of utilizing ordinary k-folds cross-validation, you must consider the fact that a time series is not randomly distributed data, but rather is ordered chronologically. Even if the impact doesn't persist in the early years, if a pattern arises in later periods, your model may still detect it!

You'll want to use forward chaining, which allows you to model on historical data before looking at current data.

fold 1: training [1], test [2]

fold 2: training [1 2], test [3]

fold 3: training [1 2 3], test [4]

fold 4: training [1 2 3 4], test [5]

fold 5: training [1 2 3 4 5], test [6]

How do you prune a decision tree?

Pruning is the process of removing branches from a decision tree model that have low predictive power to minimize the model's complexity and improve its prediction accuracy. Pruning can be done from the bottom up or from the top down, using techniques like reduced error pruning and cost complexity pruning.

Replacing each node is the simplest form of reduced error trimming. If it doesn't reduce expected accuracy, keep it pruned. This heuristic is quite near to a strategy that would optimize for maximum accuracy, despite its simplicity.

How do you deal with data that is missing or corrupted in a data set?

In a data set, you could identify missing or corrupted data and decide to remove those rows or columns or replace them with another value.

Isnull() and dropna() are two highly important Pandas methods for finding columns of data with missing or corrupted data and dropping those values (). The fillna() method can be used to replace invalid data with a placeholder value (for example, 0).

What would you do if you had an unbalanced data set?

When 90% of the data in a classification test falls into one category, you have an imbalanced data set. This causes issues: a 90% accuracy can be distorted if you don't have any predictive power on the other category of data! Here are some strategies for getting over the hump:

1. Collect new data to balance out the data set's imbalances.
2. Try a completely different algorithm on your data set.

What matters is that you have a good understanding of the harm that an uneven data set might create and how to correct it.

Have you used Spark or other big data machine learning tools before?

You should familiarize yourself with the meaning of big data for various businesses and the many technologies they will require. Spark is the most popular big data technology right now, as it can handle massive data sets quickly. If you don't have expertise with the tools required, be honest, but also check at job descriptions to see what tools are mentioned: you'll want to devote time to learning about them.

Model and Feature Selection

What is the difference between a discriminative and a generative model?

A generative model will learn data categories, but a discriminative model will learn the differences between different data categories. On classification problems, discriminative models will typically outperform generative models.

Model correctness or model performance: which is more essential to you?

This quiz will put your machine learning model performance knowledge to the test! The specifics are typically the subject of machine learning interview questions. How does it make sense that models with higher accuracy would have lower predictive power?

It has everything to do with the fact that model correctness is merely a subset of model performance and a potentially deceptive one at that. If you intended to detect fraud in a large data set with a sample size of millions, for example, a more accurate model would most likely predict no fraud at all if only a small percentage of cases were fraudulent. This, on the other hand, would be useless for a predictive model—one that claimed there was no fraud at all! Model correctness isn't the be-all and end-all of model performance, thus questions like this assist you to demonstrate that you grasp that.

What is the Formula One score? What would you do with it?

The F1 score is a metric measuring how well a model performs. It's a weighted average of a model's precision and recall, with outcomes ranging from 1 to 0, with 1 being the greatest and 0 being the worst. It'd be used in categorization exams where genuine negatives aren't as important.

When is it better to use classification instead of regression?

Classification yields discrete values and data organized into rigid categories, but regression yields continuous findings that make it easier to discriminate between individual points. If you want your results to reflect the belongingness of data points in your data set to particular specified categories, you should use classification rather than regression (e.g., if you wanted to know whether a name was male or female rather than just how correlated they were with male and female names).

Give an example of when ensemble approaches could be beneficial.

To improve predictive performance, ensemble approaches combine a number of learning algorithms. They usually help models become more robust by reducing overfitting.

You may give some instances of ensemble methods, such as bagging, boosting, and using a "bucket of models" method, and show how these can improve predictive power.

How do you tell if you're overfitting a model?

This is a straightforward reiteration of fundamental concern in machine learning: the risk of overfitting the training data and carrying the noise into the test set, resulting in inaccurate generalizations.

To avoid overfitting, there are three basic methods:

1. By employing fewer variables and parameters, you can reduce variance in the model by removing some of the noise from the training data.
2. Use techniques like k-folds cross-validation for cross-validation.
3. Use regularization techniques like LASSO to punish particular model parameters that are prone to overfitting.

What methods of evaluation would you use to assess the efficacy of a machine learning model?

The data set would initially be partitioned into training and test sets, and then cross-validation techniques would be used to further segment it into composite sets of training and test sets within the data. After that, you should compile a comprehensive set of performance metrics. The F1 score, accuracy, and confusion matrix could all be utilized as indicators. It's critical that you demonstrate that you understand the nuances of how a model is tested and how to use relevant performance measurements for various circumstances.

What criteria would you use to assess a logistic regression model?

A chunk of the previous question is repeated here. You must demonstrate that you grasp the common aims of logistic regression (classification, prediction, and so on), as well as present some examples and application cases.

Deep Learning

What exactly is deep learning and how does it differ from other machine-learning algorithms?

Deep learning is a subfield of machine learning that deals with neural networks and how to utilize backpropagation and neuroscience principles to model massive quantities of unlabeled or semi-structured data more effectively. Deep learning, in this sense, is an unsupervised learning technique that use neural nets to learn data representations.

What is deep learning and why is it important? What is the advantage of doing so?

Because deep learning networks excel at unsupervised learning, they avoid the drawbacks of machine learning. The main distinction between supervised and unsupervised learning is that unsupervised learning does not label data. If you were developing an image recognition network, for example, deep learning networks could learn to detect cats even if the photographs didn't come with the label "cat."

You can imagine how valuable it is in real-world applications to be able to learn from unlabeled or unstructured data. It helps you to create systems that can learn from a chaotic and unpredictably changing environment using a range of inputs.

What are the different types of architecture?

Because most deep learning algorithms use neural network designs, deep learning models are sometimes referred to as deep neural networks.

Convolutional neural networks are one of the most popular types of deep neural networks (CNN or ConvNet). A CNN combines learned features with incoming data and employs 2D convolutional layers, making it ideal for processing 2D data like photos.

CNN's do away with the requirement for manual feature extraction, so you won't have to figure out what features are used to classify images. The CNN operates by extracting features from photos directly. The required features are not pre-trained; instead, they are discovered when the network trains on a set of images. Deep learning models are particularly accurate for computer vision applications such as object categorization thanks to this automated feature extraction.

Among the other networks are:

- Unsupervised Pretrained Networks (UPNs)
- Recurrent Neural Networks
- Recursive Neural Networks

What steps would you take to develop an image recognition system?

On a high level, it appears to be:

- The data set is being collected.
- Splitting the data set and importing libraries
- CNN Architecture
- Full connection
- Improvement of data

- Training
- Testing

How would you go about constructing a time series network?
It goes like this:

- Univariate time series forecasting.
- Multivariate time series forecasting.
- Multi-step time series forecasting.

Regularization

What is the difference between L1 regularization and L2 regularization?

L2 regularization spreads error across all terms, whereas L1 regularization is more binary/sparse, with several variables allocated a 1 or a 0 in weighting. Setting a Laplacean prior on the terms corresponds to L1, whereas setting a Gaussian prior relates to L2.

What exactly is a dropout?

A dropout is a regularization approach invented by Google that prevents complex co-adaptations on training data, reducing overfitting in neural networks.

By randomly dropping out nodes during training, a single model can be utilized to simulate having a huge variety of distinct network designs. It's a remarkably successful regularization strategy for reducing overfitting and improving generalization error in deep neural networks of all kinds, and it's incredibly computationally cheap.

Clustering

What is the definition of distortion function? Is it a convex or a non-convex surface?

The k-means clustering distortion function is a simple sum of squared distances that indicates how well data fits into a cluster:

$$I_j = \sum_{t=1}^{N_j} [d(x_{jt}, w_j)]^2$$

We add the squared distances from all cluster points x to the cluster center w for a particular cluster j. For a given value of K, the total distortion is just the sum of all distortions:

$$S_K = \sum_{j=1}^{K} I_j$$

The scree plot shows how total distortion varies as K is increased. When K equals the number of samples in the data set and each point in the data set belongs to its cluster, the total distortion is zero at the limit. This is a non-convex function.

Describe the EM algorithm in detail?

The EM technique finds maximum-likelihood estimates for model parameters when you have incomplete data. The "E-Step" finds probabilities for data point assignment based on a set of hypothesized probability density functions, whereas the "M-Step" updates the original hypothesis with new data. The procedure is repeated until all of the parameters have stabilized.

Natural Language Processing (NLP)

What exactly is WORD2VEC?

Text is processed using WORD2VEC, a two-layer neural network. It takes a text corpus as input and outputs a set of vectors containing feature vectors for each word in the corpus. While Word2vec isn't a deep neural network, it does convert text to a numerical format that deep neural networks can understand. Deeplearning4j is a Java and Scala library that implements a distributed version of Word2vec that runs on Spark and GPUs.

Word2vec has many uses than only processing sentences in the wild. Genes, code, likes, playlists, social media graphs, and other verbal or symbolic series in which patterns can be recognized can all be used. More wonderful reading and in-depth information about WORD2VEC may be found here.

What exactly is t-SNE? Why would you choose PCA over t-SNE?

t-SNE (t-Distributed Stochastic Neighbor Embedding) is a non-linear dimensionality reduction approach that is especially well suited for the presentation of high-dimensional data sets. It is widely used in image processing, natural language processing (NLP), genetic data, and speech processing.

The following is how it works:

- The algorithm begins by calculating the probability of point similarity in high-dimensional space and the probability of point similarity in the equivalent low-dimensional space. The conditional probability that a point A would choose point B as its neighbor if neighbors were chosen in proportion to their probability density under a Gaussian (normal) distribution centered at A is used to compute point similarity.
- For a perfect representation of data points in lower-dimensional space, it then tries to minimize the difference between these conditional probabilities (or similarities) in higher-dimensional and lower-dimensional space.
- t-SNE uses a gradient descent approach to minimize the sum of Kullback-Leibler divergence of overall data points to quantify the minimization of the sum of the difference of conditional probability.

Loss Optimization

Identify some common regression loss functions. Contrast and compare Mean square error, quadratic loss, L2 loss.

The most frequent regression loss function is mean square error (MSE). The sum of squared distances between our target variable and predicted values is known as MSE. Mean absolute error, L1 loss: Another loss function used in regression models is mean absolute error (MAE). The MAE is the total of our target and anticipated variables' absolute differences. It calculates the average magnitude of mistakes in a group of forecasts without taking into account the directions of the errors.

Huber loss, also known as smooth mean absolute error, is less sensitive to data outliers than squared error loss. At 0 it's also differentiable. It's essentially absolute error, which when little becomes quadratic. The size of the error required to make it quadratic is determined by a hyperparameter, (delta), which can be adjusted. When 0 and MSE are equal, Huber loss approaches MAE (large numbers).

One of the major drawbacks of utilizing MAE for neural net training is its continual huge gradient, which can result in missing minima at the conclusion of gradient descent training. Gradient drops as the loss approach its minimum in MSE, making it more exact. In such circumstances, Huber loss can be extremely useful because it curves around the minima, lowering the gradient. It's also more resistant to outliers than MSE. As a result, it incorporates the best features of both MSE and MAE. The issue with Huber loss is that it is possible that we will need to train the hyperparameter delta, which is an iterative process.

What is the definition of the 0–1 loss function? Why can't the 0–1 loss function, often known as classification error, be used to optimize a deep neural network?

A popular loss function used in classification learning is zero-one loss. For a correct classification, it assigns a loss of 0 and for a wrong classification, it assigns a loss of 1. Convexity is the reason it isn't a good fit as a loss function for optimization. At 0, it is non-convex and non-differentiable. As a result, even if you use a derivative to make the function differentiable, the function will still be non-convex and difficult to optimize. Convex functions, such as the hinge loss in conjunction with the SVM model, are a superior alternative.

Monte Carlo Methods

What are Monte Carlo algorithms, and how do they work?

Monte Carlo (MC) methods are a subset of computational algorithms that make numerical estimates of unknown parameters via a process of repeated random sampling. The technique identifies all possible consequences of your decisions and evaluates risk.

What are deterministic algorithms, and how do they work?

For a given input, deterministic algorithms will always create the same output and cycle through the same stages. Because they can run quickly on computers, deterministic algorithms are the most common and practical sort of algorithm. In the case of non-deterministic algorithms, the compiler may provide different results for the same input in different runs. Non-deterministic algorithms, on the other hand, are incapable of solving the issue in polynomial time or anticipating the next step.

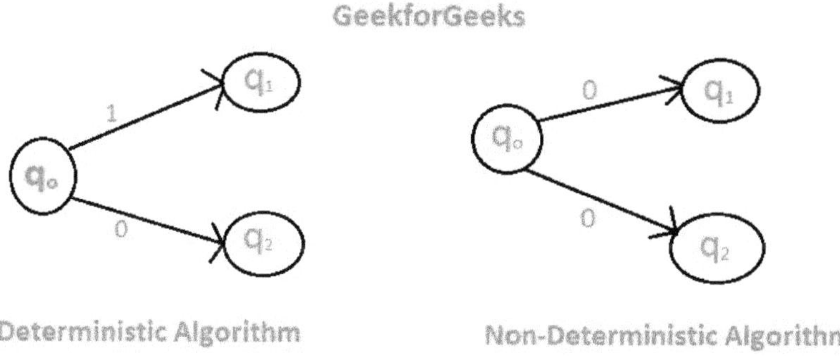

Representation

What is representation learning, and how does it work? What is the benefit of it?

Representation learning is the process of learning representations of incoming data, usually by modifying it, to make a job like classification or prediction easier. Different representations can be learned in a variety of ways. Consider the following example:

- The goal of learning a representation that captures the probability distribution of the underlying explanatory features for the observed input in probabilistic models is to learn a representation that captures the probability distribution of the underlying explanatory features for the observed input. After that, the learned representation can be utilized to make predictions.
- The representations in deep learning are created by composing many non-linear transformations of the input data with the purpose of

producing abstract and usable representations for tasks such as classification and prediction.

It's helpful since models are reliant on the presentations they learn to provide. It is useful in deep learning because representation allows a complicated block to transform an input into a rich representation, requiring only a single layer to do task-specific preparation (in using BERT for NLP tasks, for example). The model generates input representations that can be used for a variety of NLP applications. Furthermore, knowing how different representations are useful for different tasks can help practitioners better comprehend different deep learning model designs.

What are the trade-offs that representation learning must take into account?

There is a trade-off in most representation learning problems between preserving as much input information as possible and achieving pleasant qualities

Dimensionality Reduction

Give instances to illustrate the plague of dimensionality. Why are dimensionality reduction techniques required?

The number of configurations can expand exponentially as the dimensionality of the features space increases, and thus the number of configurations covered by an observation decreases. In general, the more data we have, the more processing power we'll require, and we'll also need more training data to build a useful model.

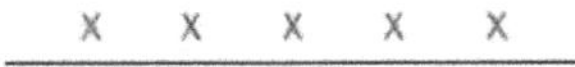

Five data points in a one-dimensional feature space

There are 25 data points in a two-dimensional features space.

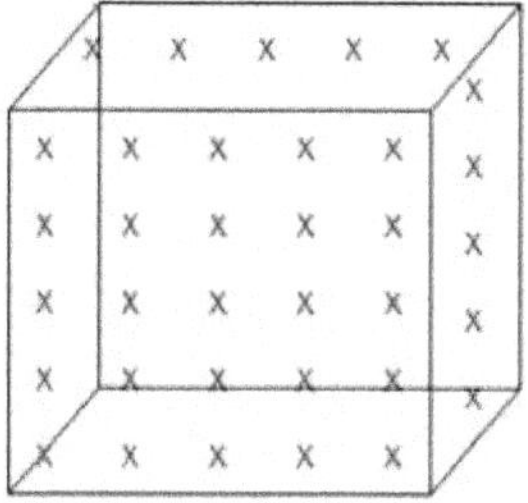

There are 125 data points in a three-dimensional features space.

As you can see, if you can reduce dimensionality, you can save money. Dimensionality reduction is a technique for compressing data without losing too much signal.

Interest and Understanding of ML

What are the most recent papers you've read on machine learning?

If you want to show interest in a machine learning position, you should keep up with the newest scientific research on the subject. This summary of deep learning in Nature by the scions of deep learning (from Hinton to Bengio to LeCun) is an excellent example of the type of publication you should credit.

Do you have any machine learning research experience?

Most companies looking for machine learning jobs will look for it in addition to your academic education in the field. Research papers co-authored or overseen by subject experts might represent the difference between getting hired and not getting hired. If you don't have any formal research experience, prepare a description of your research experience and papers, as well as an explanation for your lack of formal research experience.

What are some of your favorite examples of machine learning models in action?

Some examples may be found in the Quora thread above, such as decision trees that classify people into different cognitive levels based on IQ scores. Make sure you have a few instances in mind and that you can express what spoke to you. You must show that you're interested in how machine learning works.

What method do you believe Google is using to train data for self-driving cars?

This and other machine learning interview questions put your knowledge of different machine learning approaches to the test, as well as your ingenuity if you don't know the answer. Recaptcha is being used by Google to collect tagged data from stores and traffic signs. They're also using data gathered by Sebastian Thrun at Google X, some of which was obtained by his graduate students driving buggies over the desert sands!

How would you model AlphaGo's strategy for defeating Lee Sidol in Go?

In the history of machine learning and deep learning, AlphaGo defeating Lee Sidol, the top human Go player, in a best-of-five series was a watershed moment. "Monte-Carlo tree search with deep neural networks that have been taught by supervised learning, from human expert games, and by reinforcement learning from games of self-play," according to the report.

Case Studies/Scenarios

These are more particular examples that a corporation may provide you with that are relevant to their industry.

What are your thoughts on our current data collection procedure?

This type of question demands you to pay close attention and provide helpful and informative feedback. Your interviewer is attempting to determine whether you'd be a valuable member of their team, as well as whether you understand the complexities of why certain items in the company's data process are configured the way they are based on the company- or industry-specific variables. They want to see if you can hold your own intellectually. Act following this.

How can we make money with your machine learning skills?

This is a difficult question to answer. The perfect response would demonstrate an understanding of the business's driving forces and how your abilities might be applied. If you were interviewing for a job at Spotify, for example, you could say that your ability to design a stronger recommendation model would boost user retention, which would lead to increased income in the long run.

The startup metrics listed above can assist you in determining which performance indicators are critical for startups and tech companies as they consider revenue and growth.

Product Management Skillsets

Here are some critical questions and suggestions from Rafi Lurie's excellent prep sheet. I haven't gone into specific solutions because they are much more open-ended, but check out the guide for more information on how to approach these issues.

Design a washing machine for those who are blind.

- Next, create a laundromat with all of those washing machines and describe the experience from the moment you enter until you depart.

What product do you feel has a lot of potentials but hasn't achieved it yet? Why? What would you build to help this product become successful?

Conceptualizing, designing, and building a new feature is only half the battle. How do you launch a new feature? How does it get incorporated into the existing product?

Does that stay stable over time or does this feature change throughout a user's lifetime? How would you spread awareness about your product?

Managers Expectation

To provide you with a wide overview of the many sorts of interviews, we interviewed hiring managers from startups, software firms, and large enterprises.

Furthermore, each of these managers has a distinct function to play and hires for different types of individuals. They should offer you a good idea of what each one is looking for and how you may prepare to stand out.

What do you look for?

We look at what a candidate has done on GitHub as one of the first things we do. We're interested in seeing how active they are as a contributor and what personal projects and/or open-source projects they've worked on.

We'd also look at how junior employees performed in university projects, hackathons, and research. However, for top executives, work experience is significantly more important. We'd like to see their work with real data, not simply pre-processed data sets, as well as what they've done with it.

What is the general flow of your interview process?

It's as such for machine learning engineers:

- Resume screen
- Phone screen
- Technical interview
- Deep, technical on-site interview with a product on-site interview

What is the finest piece of advice you can provide job seekers?

My greatest advice is to work on projects often and make them public on your GitHub page.

Also, concentrate on real problems using real data, because most problems in the real world lack flawless data. You'll spend the majority of your time cleaning up data. You must be able to demonstrate that you can complete the entire pipeline, from data engineering through modeling to code generation.

What are the most important questions you ask? Is there anything special about it?

We'd ask queries like these when it came to technical issues:

- When was the last time you used a data set, and what did you do with it?
- In certain instances, we'll inquire as to why you choose one model over another. What are the advantages and disadvantages?
- Can you describe how you arrived at your conclusions? How do you go about validating a model?
- What does what you discovered has to do with anything?

We'd like to observe your thought process for non-technical questions:

- What are your strategies for dealing with ambiguity?
- How do you decide what to work on, rather than just how to work on it?
- Are you aware of the business consequences and impact of what you're working on?

What do you look for in your tests?

Finally, we're looking for machine learning literacy, as well as the capacity to use what you've learned in the classroom to complete the process and a real interest in ML and AI outside of work.

We look for people who have the same DNA as us and who are really interested in working with us. We also need to know if a candidate is okay with the ambiguity and fast speed of a startup. Love people, establishing trust, focusing on the effect, taking action, and being present are our core values.

We're not looking for a one-size-fits-all profile. Hiring for these positions used to include "finding someone with a Ph.D. in San Francisco". But now things are a little different. Nowadays, everyone and their mother refer to themselves as data scientists or machine learning scientists. As a result, we must delve further. We look for diversity from a variety of perspectives. Yes, our researchers have Ph. D.s, but they don't have to be in data or statistics: one of our engineers has a Ph.D. in astrophysics and has worked on black hole research.

What is the general outline of your interviewing procedure?

Step 1: Call a machine learning recruiter for 30 minutes.

- Discuss the projects on which you've worked and the influence you've had.
- What exactly did you do to make that happen?
- What would it take for you to be content at work?

Step 2: Phone interview with a member of the machine learning team for 45 minutes.

- Interview on a shared screen.

- Writing code with one of the team members in real-time (typically in Python).

Step 3: In-person interview (three to four hours)

- Values and behavior
- This might even be done with an entry-level employees if they are well-versed in the company's ideals.
- Three 45-minute technical interviews, typically with three separate people
- Every interviewer will have a different point of view on the candidate.
- We'll look at how to put systems, data structures, and algorithms together.
- Candidates do not have to hit a home run in all three, but they must perform admirably in each.

Take note of the following:

- We don't allow the talents and values of the interviewers to mix.
- This helps us to reach out to applicants we might not have reached out to otherwise.
- The hiring committee will convene at the end of that day or early the following day.
- Despite the fact that it is a lengthy process, we are able to make an offer within 24-48 hours.

What is your finest piece of advice?

In our interview process, the best advice we can give is to be vulnerable and demonstrate your humanity. That's just as important to us as your machine learning talents.

What do you look for in your tests?

The behavioral abilities and values make up half of our interview process. The second half of the job entails whiteboarding solutions to unclear problems, which is frequently done in Python. We look for coding skills, which we usually do in Python. We're also concerned about data software abilities, such as the ability to make sense of and communicate findings concerning ambiguous data.

Another Hiring Manager

We are an oncology-focused health technology firm. To progress cancer research, we use data. We are hiring analysts, data scientists, and software engineers for a product-focused data science team. They're concentrating on data-driven product discovery and data-driven decision-making.

What is the general flow of your interview process?

1. The first step is usually a cold analytical exercise in which you are given a data set and asked to answer a few questions.
2. Then we'll undertake a phone/Zoom screen to see if you have any analytical skills and to get to know you and your work. We'll question you about one or two projects in your portfolio that you've completed. The majority of the interview is then devoted to an open-ended exercise designed to assess your data modeling and data analytical abilities.
3. We look at your ability to take something that is vaguely framed and put it into a business or product perspective, in addition to your technical skills. We're curious as to how much information you can provide when considering the user.

You arrive on-site after finishing the screen and speak to four or five different groups.

One focuses on your ability to think about products. We'd offer you a couple of interesting open-ended product concepts and encourage you to speak about how you'd priorities different options and trade-offs. The next step is a coding interview, in which you will be asked to whiteboard a coding problem.

The third activity is cross-functional collaboration. We operate in very cross-functional teams because of the nature of our work, with everyone from medical specialists, oncologists, and data analysts on the same team, side by side, as well as people that are typical of a digital firm, such as a product manager. Everyone has a unique mix of skills, and it's critical for us to understand how you could work in and communicate across various departments. This form of the interview focuses on behavioral questions to examine how you can communicate with someone from a different background across your space.

The fourth exercise is a bit of a risky proposition. We either give you data science or a data modeling interview, depending on your skillset and career plan. Modeling focuses on data modeling, SQL, and analytical skills, as well as how good you are at them. The more statistical machine learning methodology is used in data science.

What is the best piece of advice you can give?

Make sure you understand the fundamentals. Many individuals are obsessed with machine learning and deep learning buzzwords. Depending on where you're going, we don't construct large-scale systems or focus on the challenges that Facebook or Google do, at least not with us. However, for us, it's about comprehending and putting an open-ended business challenge into the domain of an analyst. Take a business problem and figure out how to use data to solve it.

What are the most important questions you ask? Is there anything special about it?

We're interested in seeing if you can redirect questions to the client and keep the end-user in mind. We aren't overly concerned about technological details. What does it take to be an MVP? What would it look like if the resources were doubled? What criteria do you use to assess your success? And how well do you respond to criticism?

What do you look for in your tests?

We value cross-functional employees who are also product experts. We also have a "reverse interview" process in which candidates can plan meetings with various members and functions of our team to have a better understanding of what's going on. It is critical for us.

Selected Candidate's Interview Questions

What shocked you the most, and what did you find the most challenging?

Any of the interview questions didn't surprise me in the least. During the interview process, I discovered that it was extremely behavioral and that a lot of it was about my personal experiences and perspectives; for example, "What do you think about machine learning and product development?"

To be clear, they did ask a lot of product-related questions as well. Even though I was interviewing for a machine learning position, there weren't many questions about machine learning. "Tell me about a moment when..." was a common refrain in the interview, and you would change your response accordingly.

"Tell me about a moment when you argued with an engineer," for example. In my case, I had a disagreement with an engineer when a machine learning system we were working on together made poor recommendations. We overreacted at first, only to discover that we had not created it traditionally. So we took a step back, made amends, and moved forward with a better working relationship.

What advice would you provide to someone who wants to ace the interview?

Recognize whether or not a given application or problem is a decent ml candidate for interview questions. It's crucial to know which applications and challenges are strong candidates for machine learning in preparation for the interview. Many situations do not necessitate the use of machine learning. Furthermore, there are situations when using machine learning may be harmful to the problem you're attempting to solve.

When confronted with an interview problem, the most important thing to ask oneself is "could I achieve 80% of my needs with a rules-based model?" Using rules-based models has three major advantages:

1. Models based on rules are less expensive. It takes less time to construct them.
2. Because your code and construct the logic, rules-based models are easier to troubleshoot.

3. Some user behavior benefits from being predefined. When a user, for example, do X, Y happens. It's more reliable.

You'll be working at Kite in no time. What made you want to work there in the first place?

I wanted to work on a project where machine learning was a big part of the solution. There isn't enough electricity to run a side feature. This company's entire product is based on machine learning.

The team's expertise in machine learning is the second reason. You want to learn from the finest and learn the best practices.

Another Hiring Manager

What advice would you provide to someone who wants to ace the interview?

My recommendation is that you prepare thoroughly for the coding portion of the interview.

Your method counts a lot, and the purpose of the interview is to show off your work.

Of course, you'll need to be well-versed in statistics and machine learning. And knowing the strategies and answers isn't enough; you also need to know them intuitively. Knowing how to do math is beneficial.

You should expect to be interviewed by commercial stakeholders as well as technical ones. However, regardless of who is conducting the interview, keep in mind that you are there to address a business problem. Remember to treat everyone with respect, from the receptionist to the last person you speak with.

How did your job interview go?

- This was a phone screen to see whether I was a good fit for the company and to ask about my recent experience.
- Then we had a data set as a take-home challenge.

- Interview with a senior data scientist about technical matters.

  ○ We went over machine learning questions at this point. It was at this point that the difficult questions became obvious.

  ○ The most crucial component was connecting my response to my experience.

My general impressions of the interview process are as follows:

1. In-person communication is far more intimate. It's simpler for you to assess the other person's personality. Ultimately, they want to get to know you as a person, despite the technical questions. You can evaluate the company better in person, in my opinion. If you're working remotely, make sure to inquire about the company's latest projects.
2. Consider the following inquiries:

   a. What would I do if I were allowed to join the team?
   b. How are ML projects managed? Are they planned out?
   c. Do you have any agile processes in place?
   d. What are the normal working hours?
   e. How does the team stay up to date on what's going on in the field? A Friday reading group, for example, exists at some of the companies where I've worked.
   f. When working on a project as a data scientist, who would I report to?

Another Hiring Manager

What shocked you the most, and what did you find the most challenging?

The job description may or may not match the position for which you are interviewing. I had intended to apply for a more generalist role, but there was an NLP-specific challenge on the whiteboard at one point. I would have prepared for an NLP issue if I had known there would be one for this role. Many firms and their job postings are susceptible to this.

Integrate surprised me by having a lot of value elements, which I thought was fantastic. That is something that not many businesses do. It was critical to ensure that my ideas did not contradict those of the organization.

What advice would you provide to someone who wants to ace the interview?

A lot of whiteboarding is going on in this room. Expect a lot of open-ended questions on creating solutions to a challenging problem as a result. You have the option of designing a solution based on your math and foundation. It's conceivable they didn't speak with the same person. The end consequence, though, will be the same.

If you can acquire more particular preparation from the organization without receiving the actual questions, that will assist you in your preparation.

"Hey, I'm usually a generalist, so it's quite beneficial for me to know what specific challenges and ML areas I can focus on for the interview," I'd say in the script. I'd also inquire about the types of numbers and issues they're dealing with as a company. Gaining knowledge in this area will assist you in determining the best way to prepare.

Searching at anything too narrowly in an interview like this can lead to missing the big picture, the main values, and the main elements that a person is looking for. I came from a more theoretical background in my situation. Going into machine learning, there was a bias against me, with people believing I was more of an academic than a developer. If you have a strong theoretical or statistical background, you may find yourself in this situation.

Also, demonstrate your ability to code by converting a mathematical issue into production-ready code. You'll have a greater chance if you have more examples of items and projects that you've worked on.

On the behavioral side, the best advice I can give you is to just be yourself. Because you can't fake it many times if you have multiple behavioral interviews. Maintain a humble demeanor while demonstrating your inquisitiveness. Show your humanity by being vulnerable and real.

What made you decide on your current position?

Because of the interview procedure, I chose this job. The folks I met along the way were incredible. Throughout, they made me feel like a human being.

What about the interview surprised you, and what did you find challenging?

I expected a project that focused solely on machine learning techniques, but instead, the project described even the most basic code and didn't seem to care much about the algorithm itself. They were more interested in the pre-analysis and my strategy to solve the data science problem. They weren't expecting something particularly complicated or precise. It took me by surprise.

Another thing that shocked me during the interview was how satisfied they were with the manner I did a pre-analysis after cleaning the data. That impressed them more than simply implementing the machine learning algorithm. They were interested in seeing if I could locate the proper inputs ahead of time.

What advice would you provide to someone who is preparing for an interview?

Before diving into the algorithm, gather data and conclude. After cleaning the data, you can play around with it to see what insights you can uncover (e.g., a correlation chart). It's a straightforward analysis that may be completed without the use of any software. You can also share that with clients to quickly pique their interests.

Go in with confidence. Your skills will be in great demand, even if you're new to data science or machine learning. Recognize how valuable you are. It's also not only, "Do you know everything there is to know about algorithms?" They're more interested in your mental process and how you respond to particular questions.

What factors played a role in your decision to take this position?

It appeared to be quite thrilling! I was going to be the company's first data scientist, bringing data-driven solutions to the table. It was a very nimble and adaptable corporation with several learning chances.

In addition, the job appeared to be an excellent one. It would help me advance in my career.

CHAPTER SIX

Takeaways

The following are the essential takeaways for a machine learning interview:

1. If you have a question about a fundamental topic, don't assume it will go unanswered. Brush up on technical principles before going through the interview process.
2. Make sure you're ready for the behavioral interview. Companies value your communication skills and ability to work well with potential coworkers just as much as you're coding abilities and knowledge of machine learning.
3. Prepare a collection of stories to share. Create a portfolio, especially if you're using GitHub. Prepare to tell a story about who you are and why your hobbies and abilities are so relevant to the organization you're interviewing with. You will be considered a candidate deserving of moving on to the next phase if you have relevant projects and are extremely clear about what you contributed to those efforts.
4. Patience is required. An interview can take a long time to complete. You should expect to have to wait.

After the Interview, What Should You Do?

You may believe that your work is done once you've completed your machine learning interview. That is not always the case.

Following is a list of things you may do after the interview to ensure that you make the greatest possible impression on your potential employers.

As a follow-up, send a thank-you note

Following up on an interview can mean the difference between internal supporters battling for your admission and disinterest. It is now standard practice to send a thank-you note. You won't want to send a boilerplate "thank you for the chance" email to an office worker who receives an average of 121 emails every day. Make an effort to be remembered. The bare minimum is a polite email. Candidates that go above and above by submitting handwritten notes or a list of views following the interview will stand out among the 120 emails received.

Let us know what you think about a topic that came up during the conversation

Going above and beyond merely expressing gratitude is a simple approach to set yourself apart. Remember what transpired during the interview and make an effort to elicit some of the problems the employer is attempting to tackle. If any of the interview's example problems are geared toward a technical direction, or if a question implies a divide between different teams, you should make a note of it and give detailed responses.

After all, an interview is more than a test; it's also a conversation. You will know exactly what challenges the organization is having if you listen carefully to the questions and ask the proper questions yourself. Why not send your ideas for solutions you'd want to pursue?

Send relevant work/homework to the employer

It can be tough to imagine how your skills could be applied in the office, especially if you have only recently met someone. The most astute hiring companies will frequently provide you a sample problem to answer that is based on real-world situations. This gives you the opportunity to show how your efforts could have a good impact on the company. Organizations that fail to do so will be hesitant to hire the best candidate since they haven't proved how they would make a positive influence on the firm. You can, however, be proactive and follow up on what you learned in the interview. You don't have to limit yourself to providing them thoughts that demonstrate that you paid attention; you may also provide them with genuine, tangible remedies.

Because she didn't have a portfolio, the author of this Forbes piece was told she couldn't get a job as a freelance copywriter because she didn't have one. The applicant realized that a significant project (the redesign of a website) was just around the corner after paying close attention throughout the interview. Instead of accepting defeat, she gave ten free website banner headline choices. Because of her initiative, she was hired to write the rest of the website's material.

You should have a portfolio that demonstrates your ability to make a difference, but sometimes that isn't enough. You can identify a business problem or an ML opportunity for the organization if you're perceptive and ask the correct questions. It's why they're recruiting in the first place: there's always something! There's a project that everyone wants to see completed or a vexing problem that no one can solve. Send them a strategy for how you'd use or play with some of the information they've provided, and then give them some good insight into your work process. It will take a lot of initiative to obtain you an offer.

Keep in touch in a professional manner

One of the most awkward parts of the post-interview process is waiting for a response. You don't want to come off as desperate by following up too many times, but companies take their time if you don't engage with them proactively. It is possible to affect the post-interview decision from outside of the company, but you should keep in mind the appropriate channel to reach somebody. Make sure to ask before the interview ends how best to reach your interviewer. Everybody has a preferred mode of communication; if they specify short emails or a call, follow that rule and dispel some of the post-interview awkwardness. As a rule of thumb, don't check in more than once every week, or better yet, in 10 days. Sometimes companies just take their time.

Make use of your connections

You should have good references from both external and internal sources, ideally. You should have strong advocates who can back your candidacy if you have been expanding your network and giving value to them. Check-in with those who suggested you internally on a regular basis, and if necessary, have them say how pleased you are to work at the company and how fortunate the organization is to have you. Hiring is frequently based on a network, and the strongest signal you can provide to a potential employer is a thriving network of individuals prepared to go to bat for you.

Accept rejection with professionalism

There's a strong probability you'll get turned down. Sometimes you're just not the right match for the job, or they've found someone who is somewhat more suitable. It's critical to keep your cool at this moment, thank the employer for their time, and move on.

People in the industry communicate amongst themselves, and acting unprofessionally at this point can only bring you poor karma and possibly cause you to be overlooked by future employers. Maintaining a professional demeanor increases the longevity of your network. What's more, a no isn't always a no. Companies will occasionally retain your information on file and contact you in the future.

"Success is the ability to move from one setback to another without losing enthusiasm," Winston Churchill famously declared. J.K. Rowling has revealed her publisher rejection letters. Airbnb's founder, Brian Chesky, has disclosed seven rejection letters from potential investors. You will have to face rejection in order to attain greatness. Everyone who has achieved success has already done so.

Keep up hope

Anxiety might be high throughout the interview process. Choosing a company to work for might help you plan your future. An interview can signal the start of a new career path. It could imply relocating cities. It's a time in our life when other people wield disproportionate power over our fates. However, as you can see from the preceding steps, you have far more control than you realize. It's critical to keep your head up and do your best.

Maintaining hope is the most crucial thing you can do during the interview process. Interviews can take a long time. It takes a long time for a company to respond to you. Before a candidate is accepted, he or she must pass a number of internal checks and processes. You may go through several rounds of interviews with the same firm without receiving a final offer. Expectations must be established. During your quest, you should never be discouraged.

How to Deal with Offers

Your goal is to receive as many offers as possible to assess and perhaps bargain. While the procedure is challenging and may take longer than you imagine, you will have earned your offers once they begin to come in. We can't stress enough how critical it is to keep your expectations in check and your hopes high.

It can take months or even a year for many candidates in the AI and machine learning sector to find the proper job, especially if they are coming from academia. Make sure you consider everything that is provided to you and choose the future that you deserve after all of your hard work.

What Should You Evaluate?

You may receive many offers if you successfully complete the interview procedure. Congratulations! Accepting a job offer entails committing a large amount of time to the organization. Keep that in mind at all times. You may use a number of elements to determine whether or not an offer is good for you.

Organizational Culture

This could be one of the most essential aspects in deciding whether or not to accept an offer. Make certain to inquire about the company's culture. Look for indicators that the company employs people who like spending time with one another; avoid generic adjectives or companies that struggle to articulate their culture, or even dismiss the subject entirely.

Great firms devote a lot of time and attention to ensuring that they hire amazing people who are passionate about what they do. That will show up in your inquiry. External and independent sources, such as corporate reviews on Glassdoor, should also be checked. To acquire their side of the story, talk to current and past employees. You'll frequently come across real-life stories that might give you a solid idea of what working at your new job would be like.

Team

The culture of a company is an extension of the people who work there, but you should like coming to work every day and working with everyone else. Make certain you're working with a team from which you can learn. You are the average of the five people with whom you spend the most time, and you'll be spending a lot of time with your coworkers.

Location

Make sure you're comfortable with the location of the organization, especially if you'll be relocating a long way to take the job. Because moving is a tough process, it's critical that you feel at comfortable in your current residence.

Salary Negotiation

According to CNBC and Glassdoor, 61 percent of employees did not negotiate their salary in their last job offer, despite the fact that those who did average saw their salary increase by 13.3 percent.

You're at a unique leverage point when you initially get your offer, which you may not see again for several years. This is the time to put your worth to the test. Make a counteroffer—a corporation will not terminate you or cancel a contract offer since you asserted your worth. Initial bids provide a margin to allow for minor discussion. Take advantage of the situation.

During a salary discussion, keep the following in mind:

1. Bring a well-researched figure that represents what you believe you're worth. Look at industry averages (mentioned below) and talk to people who work in the field to get an idea of what to expect. Never enter a negotiation without having a clear idea of what you want to get out of it.
2. Maintain a cheerful attitude and refrain from pushing too hard for what you believe you "deserve." Instead, use this as an opportunity to demonstrate your worth and the value you can add.
3. Determine your bare minimum and then ask for more. Negotiate a little bit more than you think you'll get. Any skilled negotiator will respond with a counter, and you should be ready for it.

4. Above all, don't be afraid of rejection! A firm will appreciate you being honest and upbeat throughout what is typically the most challenging portion of the recruitment process for them, as long as you maintain the process polite and professional. Make sure you understand how dedicated you are to the organization, team, and money before accepting the offer.
5. Make use of your other offers as a bargaining chip. Going into a pay negotiation with at least one additional competitive offer is always a good idea. Even if you know exactly what work you want, being able to negotiate for the remuneration you want is crucial.

It's always easier to negotiate if you have some background information about average salaries. You'll be more powerful at the negotiating table if you know more.

Although salary information is subject to change, here are some facts and numbers to get you started.

According to Indeed.com, machine learning engineers make an average of $141,000, data scientists make an average of $120,000, and product managers make an average of $140,000 at the largest IT companies. This varies by area, with the highest pay tending to be concentrated in the tech-heavy Bay Area. According to O'Reilly Media, California has the widest range and median of any state when it comes to data science. The United States has the greatest median and range of data science wages in the world, followed by the United Kingdom, New Zealand, Australia, and Canada. The lowest medians are found in Asia and Africa.

The highest-paying industries include technology and social networking companies, while education and nonprofit organizations pay the least. Salary is also influenced by the skills and tools that are employed. O'Reilly conducted a thorough investigation involving hundreds of industry members. The results of an open poll demonstrate that typical incomes are influenced by a variety of factors such as area, industry, and job title.

Visit Glassdoor for more salary information. This is also a great area to explore for more information about well-known IT companies.

What to Do After Acceptance

Congratulations if you've accepted an offer! Take a moment to exhale! You've finally achieved the end objective of this long process and landed the job you wanted, one that pays well and allows you to make a substantial social effect. Be aware that reputable businesses will go out of their way to make you as comfortable as possible. You should reach out to potential teammates to learn more about what they do and how you might assist them with their business issues. Make use of the opportunity to socialize and meet as many people as possible.

More importantly, if you have time between accepting the job and start, take it easy and enjoy it! Make the most of the opportunity to catch up with as many people as possible in your life, rest, and be thoroughly refreshed for your first day at your new company.

Conclusion

The interview process for AI and machine learning is one of the most difficult to crack, as well as one of the most competitive. Experienced engineers, Ph. D.s, researchers, or product managers will most likely be among your interviewers. And some of them will have a lot of expertise in the industry.

www.ingramcontent.com/pod-product-compliance
Ingram Content Group UK Ltd.
Pitfield, Milton Keynes, MK11 3LW, UK
UKHW021923190726
13853UKWH00002B/807

9 798885 464635